MY FAVORITE CHRISTMAS

MY FAVORITE CHRISTMAS

BY

AMY HAMMOND HAGBERG

CONTENTS

INTRODUCTION

My Grandpa Art used to sing a special song at Christmas, "Plums and Prunes and Cherries." I'm not sure if it was an original song like so many of his, but it always reminded me of the mouthwatering aromas wafting from Grandma's kitchen. Alvilda Tollefson made everything from scratch, even her daily bread.

Like so many other farmers from the prairies of North Dakota, my mother came from solid Scandinavian stock. These Americans loved their families in a no-nonsense manner and worked the land feverishly to provide for them.

That proud heritage was passed down to me and for a period of time during my adolescence, I was all about being Norwegian. I even went to a Norwegian language camp in the summer so I could learn to speak "Norsk" with Grandpa. Funny, he never could understand what I was saying. Perhaps I should have paid more attention to the teacher and less to the boys.

My grandparents usually made the grueling 400-mile road trip down to Minneapolis to celebrate Christmas with my family. I'll never forget how Grandpa pronounced it "Minaplis" in his cute little accent. They always arrived with a pack of Juicy Fruit gum at the ready and a crisp $5 bill.

Now, we weren't particularly "ethnic" during the rest of the year, but at Christmas we went all out. My mother has always been an excellent cook, and she truly spoiled us at Christmas. Much of the fare was Scandinavian: including Swedish Meatballs and the homemade lefse that Grandma always contributed to the meal. Lefse is the Norwegian version of a tortilla but is made with potatoes rather than flour. Grandma's hand-rolled lefse was by far the best on the planet. Slathered with butter and sprinkled generously with cinnamon-sugar it was nothing short of heavenly.

Now that I have kids of my own, I've worked diligently to create unique Christmas memories for them too. In addition to their regular gifts, each year we give them a special, personalized Christmas ornament; one that reflects their life or personality at the time. Each passing fancy is covered, from hockey to piano, and the kids treasure each of them. Now that they are teenagers, their collections are getting rather extensive, so when they decorate their own Christmas trees someday, they'll have a nice head start.

Something magical happens every Christmas Eve at our house, I can't quite explain it. Sometime between the candlelight service, Christmas dinner and the opening of gifts, the "Pajama Elf" visits their bedrooms and leaves a brand-new pair of Christmas pj's. I think they look forward to that surprise more than anything.

The constant stream of holiday music on the stereo, the fragrance of traditional cookies baking in the oven, the warmth of our fieldstone fireplace and the beauty of the snowy Minnesota landscape create a homespun, festive atmosphere that we all look forward to with great anticipation. Yet what we value most is the celebration of the birth of our Messiah. From the birthday cake we bake Him to the literal place of honor He has at our dinner table, Jesus is the focal point of our Christmas.

In *My Favorite Christmas*, you will enjoy a wide array of personal reflections that capture the full range of human responses surrounding the season—joy, gratitude, sorrow, lightheartedness, reconciliation, and more. In the process, our hope is that you will savor your own favorite Christmas memories—and the people who made them so special.

For God so loved the world that he gave his one and only Son, that whoever believes in him shall not perish but have eternal life.

John 3:16

JOE BONSALL

(Photo: David Johnson)

Joe Bonsall is the principal spokesman and lead vocalist for The Oak Ridge Boys, one of country music's most celebrated acts. The quartet has received nearly every award the music industry has to offer, including five Grammy Awards, four Country Music Association Awards, four Academy of Country Music Awards, and 12 Dove Awards. They have three platinum albums, ten gold albums, and have sold more than 10 million records (www.oakridgeboys.com).

I grew up in a little neighborhood of Philadelphia, Pennsylvania known as Harrowgate. We lived in a row house, and for people who aren't familiar with them, row houses are very small, compact homes common in major northeastern cities like New York, Baltimore, Boston and Philly. They are generally connected in a row down the block (hence the name), so you share a wall with

the families on either side of you. Our tiny home had two stories with a closed in front porch, a living room, a kitchen area and a few bedrooms upstairs. We also had a small, no-frills basement that housed the water heater and furnace with a very narrow staircase leading down to it.

My dad was a hard working factory guy. In fact, when I was little my parents both had to work very hard to make ends meet - like most families did back then. So we didn't have a lot. My father was also a pretty tough guy; primarily because he grew up in a very mean, awful family. His parents and brothers treated him so badly that he joined the army to get away from them. After a distinguished tour of duty, he was awarded a silver star, a bronze star and a purple heart for his service in Europe.

The enemy shot the daylights out of my father in France after he landed on Utah Beach. He was so full of metal that he could have never gone through a metal detector. The army doctors were taking shrapnel out of his body way into his seventies. Joseph Sloan Bonsall, Sr. was a veteran of World War II ... no ... my father was a *hero* of World War II.

Like so many other veterans, my father had a hard time after the war. He feared nothing, yet he had all these little hang ups that were a result of the war. One of the ways he dealt with the memories and nightmares was by drinking. Sometimes he would go off on a binge and not come home for days. Nobody ever knew where he went. He was constantly changing jobs, because no matter how good a worker you are, a factory isn't going to put up with you if you don't show up for work. His life was a mess for years, and part of my childhood was very rough because of that.

Yet despite my parents' struggles, they somehow managed to provide for me and my sister and made Christmas seem like Disneyland. I don't know how they did it. Back in those days, my parents put up the Christmas tree on Christmas Eve. When my sister and I went to bed, the house was normal. But when we woke on Christmas morning, we'd walk down the stairs and boom ... total transformation! Christmas morning was magical at our house.

One particular Christmas morning when I was about seven years old, I was absolutely blown away when I came

down the stairs. I thought I was in another world, a whole new universe! Somehow, my father had secretly built the most amazing train platform I'd ever seen. It took up half the living room! It stood at least three feet off the ground and had little metal legs to support the solid wood frame. A Lionel train set was running around the whole top of the platform spouting smoke like the real thing. He'd even built a city complete with fake grass and tiny little people. The final touch was the Christmas tree on top of the platform, fully decorated.

I had a bunch of extra presents that year, too. I remember getting an incredible Fort Apache set complete with Rusty, a little Lieutenant Rip Masters and of course, Rin Tin Tin. I remember it like it was yesterday.

It was all absolutely mind-boggling to me; I could not believe he'd gone through all of that for us. My father had built the whole train platform in the cramped basement of our row house. How he built it, how he kept it a secret, how he got it up the stairs, and later on how he got it back down the stairs, has always been a bit of a mystery to me.

When I was 15 years old, my father had a debilitating stroke. For several years after that, my buddies and I set up the platform, probably more for my mom than anything else. It took four guys and a lot of laughing to get that thing up out of the basement, into the kitchen, into the living room and then to screw the legs on and set it up like my father used to do all by himself. I'm telling you, it's huge! It was amazing to me; I just don't know how the guy did it. The U.S. won World War II because of the sheer ingenuity of the American soldier. Our young men rose up and did extraordinary things. My father was one of those extraordinary men.

I've always found it ironic that my father chose to give us such a special surprise on that particular Christmas morning, because it came when he was having some of his worst times. Perhaps it was a little way for him to say to the family, "I'm really sorry for the shortcomings, but I'm trying to do the best I can here as your dad." I know he was sorry for the times I had to get on my bicycle and go look for him in the bars. When I found him I would go home and tell my mother where he was so she could get one of the neighbors to bring him home and sober him up so he wouldn't lose his job the next day.

For years I had a strained relationship with my father because of the drinking and the sadness that brought to the household. But that Christmas morning, I knew my father really loved me because of what he did. He went the extra mile to do something special for me. It was his way of saying, "I'm having a rough time in my life, but I love my son." Later on in life I really knew it was true, but back then, as a little insecure seven year old, I really needed to know my father loved me, because sometimes I really wasn't sure.

My favorite Christmas is proof positive of a father's love for his family. During a very difficult time in his life, my father did something wonderful and selfless — something so meaningful - that it remains one of the most pivotal experiences of my life.

Time was with most of us, when Christmas Day, encircling all our limited world like a magic ring, left nothing out for us to miss or seek; bound together all our home enjoyments, affections, and hopes; grouped everything and everyone round the Christmas fire, and make the little picture shining in our bright young eyes, complete.

Charles Dickens

MEASHA
BRUEGGERGOSMAN

OPERA SINGER
(Photo: Lorne Bridgeman)

Canadian soprano Measha Brueggergosman has emerged as one of the most magnificent artists and vibrant personalities of the day. Critically acclaimed by the international press, she is the recipient of numerous national and international awards. A dynamic scope of repertoire coupled with a profound depth of artistry brings Measha Brueggergosman together with many of the finest international orchestras and most esteemed conductors of our day. In 2003, she was featured in the CBC-TV documentary, Spirit in Her Voice *(www.measha.com).*

I think the fondest memory I have to date actually happened this past Christmas. My mother worked for the federal government in computers. The irony in that is that she owned a run-down, 1980s vintage, Atari 64 piece of garbage — it literally took her all day to check email. The computer essentially took up the entire room

because the hard drive was so huge. Last year my husband and I said to each other, "This madness has to end!"

In our family, we have this great tradition. Every year, one person in the family does a scavenger hunt where they follow a series of clues throughout the house, eventually leading them to their gift. Ever since I was a little girl, my mother has written the riddles. In other words, *she* was never the one doing the scavenger hunt.

Now, my husband, Markus, is amazingly skilled at riddles, rhyming, codes and things like that, so a couple of years ago he started helping my mom write the riddles. He can come up with the most convoluted puzzles for people to solve in order to get their gifts.

So this year, we decided to give my mother the riddle even though she had already written one for the next person on the rotation. I'll never forget that day. Mother didn't know that there was another envelope on the tree besides the one she had created. When we said, "Oh, mom, there's an envelope on the back of the tree," she said, "Oh really, I wonder what that is?" When she

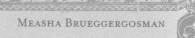

opened the envelope she was completely flabbergasted – it was the last thing she ever would have expected.

Markus wrote all these clues that rhymed and were very cryptic. My mother is extremely quick-witted and very smart, so you have to create a riddle that is quite difficult in order to stump her. The clues took her behind paintings, up to the attic, and under the bed. The final clue was all in code, and in order to decipher it she had to decode a complicated pattern Markus had written using Scripture verses from the Bible. While my mother was working out that final clue, Markus was downstairs assembling her present under the tree.

The final clue said, "Welcome to the 21st century" and brought my mother back to the living room. By the time she came down the stairs, Markus had set up the computer, attached it to the printer, and plugged it in. On the screen it said, "Merry Christmas!"

As a testament to my mother's absolute humility, she came down the stairs, looked at the computer and thought, "How nice," but never really understood that the computer was her gift. She was still looking for some wrapped present under the tree. Finally, we said, "Mom, this computer is for you," and that's when the celebration began. I can still picture this wonderful woman... she was so beside herself that she was bent over laughing, she was crying, she was jumping up and down and she was hugging everyone... all at the same time. And then she was on her knees thanking the Lord. It was the most amazing moment.

My mother is a successful woman, and she's very enthusiastic about her children, her life, her friends, and her marriage. So to see her go that extra step when something was done for her was extremely humbling. My mother very rarely likes to have the spotlight on her; she's very much a background person. I think when she acknowledged the fact that someone had seen a need she had and then responded to it, she was very touched.

For the rest of us, it was obvious that her 22-year-old computer needed to be replaced; my goodness, it still used floppy discs! But it had never occurred to her that anybody would actually replace it. God love her!

We learned that year what this familiar phrase really means, "It is better to give than to receive." That was my favorite Christmas ever.

This is Christmas: not the tinsel, not the giving and receiving, not even the carols. But the humble heart that receives anew the wondrous gift — the Christ.

Frank McKibben

JIMMY CARTER

FORMER PRESIDENT OF THE UNITED STATES
(Photo: Rick Diamond)

Jimmy Carter was the 39th President of the United States (1977–1981). After leaving office, he and his wife Rosalynn founded the Carter Center, a nonprofit organization devoted to advancing human rights and alleviating unnecessary human suffering. In 2002, President Carter won the Nobel Peace Prize for his tireless work promoting peaceful solutions to international conflicts. He is also a spokesman for Habitat for Humanity, a charity that builds houses for the needy. He is the author of numerous books, including his bestselling memoir An Hour Before Daylight *(www.cartercenter.org).*

It's not easy to choose our best Christmas, but it may have been in 1991. It involved Curtis Jackson, a black man who was born and spent his early adulthood on the farm of Rosalynn's grandfather, whom everyone called "Captain" Murray. Curtis had eight brothers

and six sisters, and he remembers the wonderful days of Christmas in their family. "We knew what we were going to get, and looked forward to it every year. It would be an apple and some dry grapes."

For a number of years, Curtis was a day laborer, and then, later, graduated to having crops of his own, which he worked "on halves." Mr. Captain furnished the mules, equipment, and land, and Curtis and his wife, Martha, did all the work and got half the crop. Martha had two children, but Curtis said "she had a weak system," and both children died as infants. The family had a monthly draw of fifteen dollars, with which they would acquire store-bought groceries, tobacco and snuff, and clothing. He said this was a lot more than the thirty dollars his daddy got each month, with fifteen children to feed.

After Mr. Captain retired from farming, Curtis got a job on a sawmill crew. He would get up each morning at four o'clock, Martha would fix his noon meal in a gallon lard can, and he would walk to the center of Plains, where a logging truck picked him up to go to a large sawmill in Dumas, about five miles west of town. There the individual

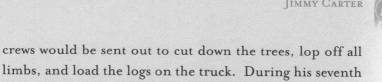

crews would be sent out to cut down the trees, lop off all limbs, and load the logs on the truck. During his seventh year there, Curtis's chain saw slipped when he was cutting limbs, and severed his right leg just above the knee.

When he could walk again, Curtis got a job as handyman at the local nursing home, which had formerly been the Wise Sanitarium, where my mother had been a nurse. He worked there another seven years, and then Rosalynn and I hired him to help me tend to our yard and keep a path cleared around our fishpond.

Curtis was a willing worker, always laughing about something, and a wonderful raconteur. He loved to describe farm life as he remembered it from his boyhood. Although we didn't know each other in those early days, he was a contemporary of mine, and we shared a lot of similar experiences. Curtis and I had long conversations, and he helped refresh my memory as I took notes that later surfaced in my book *An Hour Before Daylight*. He had a lot of trouble with his wooden leg, so one day we drove to a nearby city where he was fitted with a well-designed prosthesis. For the first time since his accident, he could

walk without pain.

When Curtis' wife, Martha, became ill, we went to visit her, and were appalled at their ramshackle house. It had no heat except for a small woodstove, we could see through the walls in several places, and there were old buckets sitting around to catch the streams of water that came through the roof when it rained. Curtis said, "It's good on clear nights. We can see the stars from our bed." Some of the sills had rotted out, and the limber floorboards bent down like a trampoline with a person's weight. In October, Martha developed what Curtis called "high blood," and had to be admitted to the nursing home.

Rosalynn and I decided that the Jacksons needed a new house, and we talked it over with the folks in our church. We were already involved with Habitat for Humanity, an organization devoted to providing decent homes for needy families. The international headquarters is in Americus, just ten miles from Plains, and Curtis and Martha easily qualified for the program.

Habitat's normal policy is that the future homeowner's

family members should put in five hundred hours of work and pay the full cost of their new house, including materials and labor. At the same time, we follow the Biblical prohibition against charging interest to a poor person. With twenty years to pay, this would keep Curtis's monthly payments low enough so he could afford them from his Social Security income. Curtis couldn't read or write, so we prepared the papers, and he helped our volunteer work crews in clearing off a site alongside his old house and preparing the foundation for the new home. Since he was physically handicapped, his wife was ill, and he had no children, some of the neighbors and volunteers helped Curtis fulfill the work requirement.

The people in Plains responded enthusiastically to our call for volunteers, and we soon had enough workers to set Christmas Eve as a target date for completion of the house. We spent the last two days and nights putting on the final touches: laying carpets and tile floors, planting shrubbery, trimming the doors and windows, installing a new stove, refrigerator, and heating system, and hanging paintings on the walls. Our children and grandchildren

who came to Plains for Christmas joined us, and we labored until dark on Christmas Eve to complete the multitude of small tasks that always confront builders at the last minute.

Then, after dark, Curtis picked up Martha and brought her home to sleep in their new house. I think it's true to say that most of us had forgotten all about Santa Claus. But Curtis and Martha hadn't.

Christmas is not a time or a season but a state of mind. To cherish peace and good will, to be plenteous in mercy, is to have the real spirit of Christmas. If we think on these things there will be born in us a Savior and over us all will shine a star, sending its gleam of hope to the world.

Calvin Coolidge

STEVEN CURTIS CHAPMAN

RECORDING ARTIST
(Photo: Kwaku Alston)

Since beginning his music career in 1987, singer/songwriter Steven Curtis Chapman has made 15 studio recordings. He has sold more than ten million records – with two certified platinum and seven certified gold. He has won five Grammy awards, an American Music Award and an astounding 50 Dove Awards (more than any other artist in history). His discography also includes 44 No. 1 radio hits. Together with his wife Mary Beth, Chapman has authored the well-known Shaoey & Dot *picture book series (www.stevencurtischapman.com).*

What I loved about Christmas when I was a kid was the excitement of it. There's no other time of year that has so much anticipation and build up. I remember waiting to see the headlights of my uncle's and grandmother's cars coming down our long gravel driveway where I grew up in Kentucky. We'd have a big

Christmas Eve gathering with family at night in our old farmhouse. Oh the gifts! There was that excitement, that anticipation, that time together as a family. Now, three little Asian darlings have that opportunity in our home.

When she was 13, our daughter Emily read about the plight of orphans in China and pleaded with my wife, Mary Beth, and me to adopt a child from that country. We resisted at first, but in the end she wore us down!

So, in 2000 we brought our new daughter, Shaohannah home; the first of our three adopted daughters from China. Her name is a combination of Chinese words that mean "laughter" and "gift of God." We are so thankful for the joy and happiness these beautiful little girls have brought to our family.

Unfortunately, there are still tens of millions of children lying in bed in orphanages somewhere dreaming that one day they might also belong to a family. For those children, Christmas only highlights what they don't have and so desperately want. In China alone, more than 36 million children are waiting and hoping for a new life in a loving home. Even in America, nearly one million children are yearning for adoptive families.

Sadly, many families want to adopt these children but the costs prove to be overwhelming. In 2001, Mary Beth and I established Shaohannah's Hope, a non-profit organization created to provide information and financial grants to families who desire to adopt. So far, we have provided grants to help make possible the placement of 500 orphans with American families.

After witnessing the miracle of adoption and helping others experience it as well, we have a whole new appreciation for the Christmas season. It's had such an impact on me, in fact, that the lyrics from the emotional title track of my latest Christmas album; *All I Really Want for Christmas* is an anthem about adoption. The song shares the story of a little boy's single wish to Santa; asking not for toys, but for a family …

> *All I really want for Christmas is someone to tuck me in,*
> *A shoulder to cry on if I lose and shoulders to ride on if I win*
> *There's so much I could ask for but there's one thing I really need*
> *All I really want for Christmas … is a family.*

Are You Ready for Christmas?

Are you willing to stoop down and consider the needs and desires of little children; to remember the weaknesses and lonliness of people who are growing old; to stop asking how much your friends love you, and to ask yourself whether you love them enough; to bear in mind the things that other people have to bear on their hearts;… to trim your lamp so that it will give more light and less smoke, and to carry it in front so that your shadow will fall behind you; to make a grave for your ugly thoughts and a garden for your kindly feelings, with the gate open? Are you willing to do these things for a day? Then you are ready for Christmas!

Henry Van Dyke

CLAY CROSSE

RECORDING ARTIST

A household name in Christian music circles, Clay Crosse has had ten #1 singles, including mega-hits I Surrender All *and* I Will Follow Christ. *He is the recipient of three Dove Awards, including the 1995 award for "New Artist of the Year." (www.claycrosse.com)*

About two years ago, I felt God laying on me to pray for more compassion in my ministry. Instead of just going to a speaking engagement or a singing opportunity and look at it as a job, I needed to truly realize that people out there have hurts and needs and I'm to bring a message of hope and be God's spokesperson.

So I really started focusing on praying about that and challenged my wife, Renee, to do the same. She often presents with me at marriage retreats and seminars. She took it to heart and spent a great deal of time in prayer as well.

Interestingly enough, God was talking to her about something completely different. One day, Renee came to me and said there was something she wanted to talk with me about. For some reason, she couldn't get the country of China out of her mind and the little girls who need help over there. As she was talking I was thinking, "Is she suggesting what I think she's suggesting?"

Now, every practical bone in me said, "Honey, that's great, I appreciate that you're feeling that way, but we just can't do it. First of all, we simply can't afford it; plus we're so busy with our work and our two daughters that we just can't do it." That's what the practical side of me would have said, but that's not what came out of my mouth. What came out of my mouth was, "Yes! Let's do this! How long does it take and what will it cost?"

Renee told me all about it; that it is a lengthy process that can take up to a year and a half and that it can run upwards of $25,000. Frankly, we didn't have that kind of money. But all practicality aside, we walked into the adoption process with great faith. It's amazing how God put China on our hearts. We truly didn't sit down and weigh other countries at all; China was the place that came to us immediately and never left.

I believe part of the reason we were so focused on China is that the country has a law permitting families to have only one child. If you have a second child there are huge financial penalties - it would be the equivalent of someone in the U.S. having to pay in the neighborhood of $200,000. Not only are the parents themselves penalized, but their coworkers are fined as well and so is their boss. The Chinese government is dead-on serious about enforcing this law.

So if a woman becomes pregnant over there and already has a child, she can either get an abortion or seek out an adoption, which isn't easy to do. A lot of the young babies are abandoned, that's their fate. That's what happened to one little girl in particular; her mom left her on the front steps of a factory in China, just before work was to start. I know she did that with a loving heart with hopes that the child would be found.

As God had it, someone did find that infant and they

immediately took her to a wonderful orphanage. That was the baby Renee and I we were to have. The entire adoption process was a family affair; our two girls, Shelby (13) and Savannah (8) were involved from the very beginning. For well over a year we talked about her and prayed for her — this child that God would place with us. She was constantly in our speech — "Sophie this, Sophie that."

In September 2005 the adoption agency sent us a picture of the most beautiful baby girl in the world. That's when we pretty much flipped out - when we finally saw her it was incredible. She had been ours in our hearts for so long that it was a wonder to see her face. We knew this was what God wanted us to do.

Somehow the money was raised, and in December we were off to China to get our new little girl. Our daughters went with us too; it was a great family experience for all of us. It's hard to put into words how incredible it was when we held that baby in our arms for the first time. And on December 15, 2005 we brought 10-month-old Sophie May Crosse home to America.

So you see, this Christmas was the best Christmas ever with this new little gift of life. Any thoughts of giving or receiving gifts were really replaced by her. She's the gift.

It is abundantly clear to all of us that Sophie is God's gift to us, and prayerfully we'll be God's gift to her as she grows up in this home.

The way to Christmas lies through an ancient gate…
It is a little gate, child-high, child-wide, and there is a password:
"Peace on earth to men of good will." May you, this Christmas,
become as a little child again and enter into His kingdom.

Angelo Patri

BILLY RAY CYRUS

ACTOR AND RECORDING ARTIST
(Photo: Keith Munyun)

Multi-platinum selling recording artist Billy Ray Cyrus is best known for his 1992 smash hit, "Achy Breaky Heart," which was the most successful country single of that year. The album it appeared on, Some Gave All, *sold over 14 million copies worldwide and held the #1 position on both Billboard charts for 17 weeks. His latest recording,* Wanna Be Your Joe, *was released in the summer of 2006. Also an actor, Cyrus played the lead role on PaxTV's (now i Television) long-running hit series,* Doc. *He currently stars with his daughter on Disney Channel's hit series "Hannah Montana" (www.billyraycyrus.com).*

My mom and dad got divorced when I was 5. Two years later my mom sold a lot of her belongings just so we'd be able to pay our bills, keep our house and have some food on the table. She also wanted me and my brother to have a couple of Christmas presents;

43

not much, maybe just a pair of tennis shoes or some jeans. That was the best my mom could do at the time.

She sold some very personal items, including the piano she'd been given by her mother. My mom played music by ear, and really had a gift and a love for the piano. Selling that instrument was the greatest gift that she could give us; it was a huge sacrifice. I vowed that someday I would make it up to her.

When I was 17 years old and still in high school, my mom cleaned houses for a living. One of the homes she cleaned had a piano and that was the only place she had an opportunity to play. One day around Christmas, I came home from school and found my mom crying. The people who owned that piano had put it up for sale and she was devastated.

Without her knowing it, I contacted the owner of that piano and told her I wanted to buy it for my mom. I had very little in savings — what money I did have I'd made cutting grass, working in people's yards, and doing little odd jobs. But that lady wanted my mom to have the piano and said she would take what I had in savings, even though it was much less than what she could have sold it to someone else for.

So I emptied out my savings and brought that piano home. My buddies and I snuck it into the house when my mom was gone and set it right next to the Christmas tree. I can still see her face when she came through the door. Her eyes got great big and we all yelled "Surprise!" But she just stood there. I finally said, "Well, come on down and play us something."

I'll never forget that moment as my mom sat down at her piano with tears in her eyes and played, "Blue Eyes Crying in the Rain" by Willie Nelson. That was a perfect Christmas morning.

The Gift

What can I give Him,
Poor as I am?
If I were a shepherd
I would bring a lamb.
If I were a Wise Man
I would do my part.
Yet what can I give Him?
I give Him my heart.

Christina Rossetti

CHARLIE DANIELS

RECORDING ARTIST

Country music legend Charlie Daniels has been making music for more than 40 years. The triple platinum selling artist has released an amazing 45 albums, including his latest release, "Songs from the Longleaf Pines" (2005). In 1979, Daniels recorded mega-hit, "The Devil Went Down to Georgia", topping both the country and pop charts and earning him a Grammy Award. Daniels also earned a coveted Dove Award from the Gospel Music Association in 1994 for his Gospel recording "The Door", five CMA (Country Music Association) Awards and three Academy of Country Music Awards, in addition to dozens of other honors. All told, he represents more than 18 million in record sales (www.charliedaniels.com).

When I think about my favorite Christmas memory, what sticks out in my mind is a Christmas when I was 4 or 5 years old. I was living close to Wilmington, North Carolina and my

grandparents lived just a little way down the road from us.

As usual, we celebrated Christmas Eve that year at their house. When we got back home, lo and behold, Santa Claus had come early. Somehow, he had magically appeared while we were at my grandparent's. I couldn't believe it! Instead of having to wait until Christmas morning to see what he'd brought me, I got a head start. And that very special Christmas, Santa brought me a toy drum!

I don't remember what I said when I saw it, but I do remember the thrill I felt. Of course I beat the head out of it in just a few days, but it was still exciting. There are very few things that I remember from that period of my life, but that one memory is something that's never gone away from me.

I have so many wonderful childhood memories of Christmases in North Carolina that I wrote a song about them.

"Carolina (I Remember You)"

Charlie Daniels, Tom Crain, Taz DiGregorio,
Fred Edwards, Charlie Hayward and Jim Marshall

One of the memories that stays on my mind
about an old southern lady that I left behind
is a ramshackle bridge where the deep river winds
and an old two-lane blacktop through the tall long-leaf pines

Carolina, Carolina
You're hard but you're hard to forget

I still remember the magnolia nights
and goosefeather snow in the gray morning light
sandspurs and puppies and red autumn leaves
and the warm lights in the clear night on a cold Christmas Eve

Carolina I knew you
before the highways got to you
and I loved you as one of your own
and I still do

Of course many of my favorite memories are built around the dinner table. Ever since I was a kid I've always eaten too much on Christmas Day. When we were in Wilmington, we went over to my grandmother's house because she loved to cook ... and loved to feed people. Now my wife and I have quite a few people come to our house for Christmas dinner. We just have this big old traditional meal with our family and friends. We always have turkey, and I make the dressing – it's the only thing I can cook.

Sometime in December, we also have a Christmas party for our employees and their families. When we started out I think we had like six kids – now I don't even know how many there are. We usually have about 80 people over, so it's a crazy time. If it gets much bigger we're going to have to move it somewhere else! Santa Claus shows up and we pass out our bonus checks that day. It kind of signifies the end of the year when we're through working for a while, and it's something I look forward to every year.

My wife really gets into Christmas; so much so that we have four Christmas trees in our home. Three of those trees have a special theme: one is a special ornament tree, decorated with things we've collected and people have given us over the years. Another is a cowboy tree, with western-themed ornaments. And one is a special angel tree with all kinds of angelic decorations. And then there's the big old traditional tree we put in the den. We have a pretty high ceiling in that room so the tree is huge. It's quite a job to decorate that one — I don't get involved much in that anymore!

Music plays a big role in our home at Christmastime as well. The Charlie Daniels Band has two albums of Christmas music out, so of course they're always close at hand at our house and usually end up on the CD player a time or two. Another one of my special favorites is Nat King Cole's Christmas record. I especially love *The Christmas Song*, "Chestnuts roasting on an open fire"... that's been part of our Christmas for a long, long time. I can hardly imagine Christmas without it; it's just become such a big part of the whole tradition. That song is so intertwined in my Christmas memories I hate to think about not having it.

Down deep I'm still just a kid at heart... I hope I never grow up so much that I can't get that "kid" kind of feeling about Christmas.

Happy, happy Christmas, that can win us back to the delusions of our childish days; that can recall to the old man the pleasures of his youth; that can transport the sailor and the traveller, thousands of miles away, back to his own fire-side and his quiet home!

Charles Dickens

JOSH DAVIS

OLYMPIC GOLD MEDALIST
(Photo: Clem Spalding)

Josh Davis represented his country twice at the Olympics. He brought home three gold medals in swimming from the 1996 Atlanta Games and two silver medals from Sidney in 2000. In 2001, a new $7 million swim center was named after him in his hometown of San Antonio, Texas. Davis divides his time between swimming, his role as a husband and father, and motivational speaking (www.joshdavis.com).

Every Christmas Eve, at 5:00 p.m., my family has a Christmas Eve service. The tradition began with about 40 people, and now more than 30 years later we have well over 100 family members at the gathering.

Over the years, the get-together has been at different locations. My fondest memories are from when we went to my Aunt Tassie's place. She had the most amazing

house loaded with antique furniture. If you ask me, it was pretty risky to trust those beautiful furnishings to a wild bunch of cousins, but we had a blast! Those were years of wonder; I was a wide-eyed kid surrounded by dozens of adults I didn't know very well. And the most amazing part was that many of them handed me an envelope containing a $5 bill!

Aunt Tassie's house was just big enough to fit 30-40 people, so after a few years we were busting at the seams and had to find another venue. Now it has grown so big that we actually use a small chapel on the university campus. There's even a party room conveniently located right next to the chapel, so after the church service we just walk across the sidewalk and celebrate.

My uncle is a priest, so at the forefront of the Davis family festivities is a church service. We go through the whole ceremony; the opening prayer, verses from the Old and New Testaments, and a reading from the Gospels. My uncle then gives a short sermon and the family has an intimate time of communion. At the conclusion of the service each year, we announce the new babies and spouses in the family.

The service has evolved into quite a production for my family. My dad does the reading, and my uncle officiates. My sister, a highly accomplished opera singer, provides the music and is accompanied by my mom who is a professional pianist and organist. She does an opening song and then sings a solo while we're all taking Communion. Her voice is so breathtaking that it brings tears to the eyes of everybody there. Finally, she does a closing song and leads us all in Christmas carols.

The children have been threatened with their very lives to be on their best behavior, so everyone is remarkably cooperative during the service. But as soon as it's over, they end up running around in the courtyard; a big grassy area outside the chapel.

After the service, we go hang out in the party room and catch up. And of course, we eat! Every family brings a dish so there's plenty of food to go around. Down here in San Antonio, Texas you always have to have tamales, a traditional Mexican entree comprised of a dough exterior with beef or chicken filling wrapped in a corn husk. Our menu is kind of a merging of Irish and Hispanic cultures.

Christmas Eve is a special time of worship and symbolism for all of us. It's such a special way to celebrate Christ's birth — worshipping alongside those we love.

Tell me the story of Jesus,
Write on my heart every word;
Tell me the story most precious,
Sweetest that ever was heard.
Tell how the angels, in chorus,
Sang as they welcomed His birth,
"Glory to God in the highest!
Peace and good tiding to earth."

Fanny Crosby

BRYAN
DUNCAN

RECORDING ARTIST

Bryan Duncan was one of the defining voices of Contemporary Christian music in the 1990s. He is a three-time Dove Award recipient and multiple nominee, and has produced over a dozen number one singles. Duncan has released 15 solo albums, including his latest endeavor, A NehoSoul Christmas *(www.bryand.com).*

I've never seen anybody else's tree look quite like ours did. I can see it now... my mom put big globs of "angel hair" all over the Christmas tree. Angel hair was this cottony, fiberglass substance that was they used to make back in the 50s. Back then there weren't so many decorating options like we have today. Mom put it all over — there was so much of it that it looked kind of like fake flocking. She even wrapped it around the lights so they would shine through with a special Yuletide glow. It was interesting, I'll give you that!

In the early days of living on my own, I was a poor, starving artist and couldn't afford to buy my own Christmas tree. If somebody else had to cut off the top of their tree because it was too big for their house, I'd take it. It was crazy, I had a fully decorated, two-foot high Christmas tree. To this day, I still use a tiny little tree, only now it is an all-white flocked Christmas tree with silver balls and red lights.

I love Christmas, I think we should have it all year round. So much so, in fact, that I usually don't take down most of my decorations. All of the original Christmas lights from my first year in this apartment are still up. I just love the colors and the lights and the flash.

My favorite Christmas memories come from the days of watching my kids get excited about Christmas. We opened our gifts on Christmas morning ... I actually considered switching to Christmas Eve because the boys were always up at 4:00 in the morning waiting with bated breath to open their gifts! But the gifts weren't even the best part. It was more fun just watching them play with the wrapping afterwards. They were so tiny, that they were literally buried in Christmas presents, leftover wrappers and packaging.

My funniest Christmas memory was the year we gave our oldest son a bicycle. He was only about six, and I don't think he'd ever actually seen a bicycle — at least it sure looked that way. As he was holding it, I told him to stand over the bike to make sure it was the right height for him. Then all he had to do was sit on the seat and put his feet on the pedals. Pretty simple right?

Well, he had no clue. Instead of standing over it like a logical person would, he literally stood on top with both feet perched on the crossbar. "What are you doing?" I said. "I didn't say stand *on* it. I said stand *over* it with one leg on either side." He totally couldn't get it!

For what seemed like hours, we went over and over how to stand over the bicycle, but he just couldn't figure it out. Who would have thought a kid could misunderstand how to get on a bicycle? We never even got to the part of teaching him how to ride it; we got totally hung up on the instruction, "stand over it." We have it on film — it would

have been a huge winner on *America's Funniest Home Videos*. It might be one of those, "you had to be there" moments, but I laugh about the whole scene to this day. And you know what? That kid still can't take direction very well! We had so much laughter that Christmas, I really treasure the memory.

Every Christmas comes with old memories, both happy and sad. To me, Christmas isn't about the big stuff. And it's not about the traditions. It's the little stuff that burns memories that will last a lifetime.

Never worry about the size of your Christmas tree.
In the eyes of children, they are all 30 feet tall.

Larry Wilde

TARIK GLENN

NFL PLAYER
(Photo: Indianapolis Colts)

Tarik Glenn is an offensive tackle for the Indianapolis Colts of the National Football League. A standout at the University of California — Berkeley, Glenn was the 19th pick of the 1997 NFL draft. He has achieved Pro Bowl honors twice, in 2005 and 2006. A consistent contributor, Glenn started 16 games in eight of his nine seasons with the team.

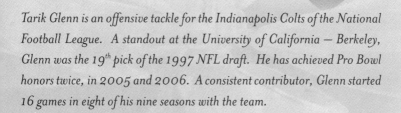

Once you're married and have a family of your own, your favorite Christmases often become the ones you have with your wife and children. But there are also those Christmases you had growing up as a kid. Oftentimes you don't remember those as clearly until you get together with your family. When you're able to put those two together and have a Christmas with both your new family and your childhood family you can have your cake and eat it too!

This past Christmas I had an opportunity to spend it with *all* of my family – my wife and three kids, my parents, my brother and even my grandmother. It was the first time all of us had been together over the holidays. I hadn't seen my dad since he'd had heart surgery in September, so spending Christmas with him and the rest of the family meant a great deal to me.

We were all so grateful he was okay. That experience allowed us to reflect on and better appreciate family relationships. And more importantly, I learned not to take time together over the holidays for granted — but was grateful for the chance to enjoy the experience with the ones I love.

For centuries men have kept an appointment with Christmas.
Christmas means fellowship, feasting, giving and receiving,
a time of good cheer, home.

W.J. Ronald Tucker

NATALIE GRANT

RECORDING ARTIST

Winner of the sought-after GMA Award (Dove) for 2006 Female Vocalist of the Year, Natalie Grant is a rising star in contemporary Christian music. She has recorded six albums, including two releases in 2005, Believe *and* Awaken, *has been included on more than nine compilations, and has had two #1 hits,* Held *and* What Are You Waiting For. *Grant has been a featured performer and speaker on the Revolve Tour and at Women of Faith events for several years (www.nataliegrant.com).*

I'm the youngest of five children. The year I turned six my family went on a road trip from our home in Seattle to visit my grandparents in San Diego for the holidays. All seven of us piled in our motor home and headed south. We even had a little miniature Christmas tree in our camper so we could have a feeling of Christmas on the road. I was so excited when I woke up every morning

and saw the little presents under the tree knowing that eventually I was going to be able to open them.

Along the way to San Diego, we stopped at a campground in northern California for the night. When we pulled into our assigned campsite and starting setting up, we couldn't help but notice the sorry-looking trailer parked in the site next to ours. It was one of those old, space-age silver trailers called an "Airstream," and it was in terrible shape... it had boarded up windows and plastic over the door and was barely holding together.

For some reason my dad, who's never met a stranger in his entire life, decided to go over and meet the people who were next to us. He found out that the father had lost his job and had five kids to support. They'd lost their home and were all actually living at the campground in that trailer. I tried to wrap my little six-year-old mind around the fact that this was somebody's permanent home. For me, being in our motor home was a blast, but I would have viewed it very differently if I'd had to live there day in and day out.

When my dad came back after meeting the people next door, he had big tears in his eyes. I remember him saying to us, "You guys, this is going to be an incredible lesson for you to learn about what Christmas is truly all about." He had us take all the food in our entire motor home; we cleaned out the fridge and cupboards, and filled all the plastic bags we could find with every last morsel of food we had. Then we took the groceries over and gave them to that desperate family.

But the sacrifice didn't end there. Dad asked each of us to take one of the presents from the tree that had our name on it and take it along to give it to the kids. Now I have to tell you that at six years of age, I wasn't very excited about that idea. I was pretty irritated actually!

I had been waiting for this special baby doll called the "Real Doll" all year long. It was amazing – you could hit a switch and the baby would eat a bottle and then it would go to the bathroom! It was all I'd been thinking about for the past twelve months. When Dad asked me to pick out a present to give away, somehow I knew I was going to end up picking that doll — the one I wanted so badly.

When I selected the box that I thought was least likely to be the Real Doll, we headed next door. But I had a plan; if their little girl opened up that package and it was my baby doll, I was going to snatch it right back out of her hands!

Well, as luck would have it when she opened up my present it was in fact the doll that I'd been dreaming of all year. But instead of snatching it back, I remember having the greatest feeling inside. It was the warmest and most genuine feeling that I had ever had up to that point in my life. That little girl stared at the doll in wonder when she realized that she got to keep it - actually got to have a present for Christmas. The kids were shell-shocked that somebody would be so kind and generous towards them. The whole experience was very cool.

To this day, I can look back and credit my dad for teaching me the true spirit and meaning of Christmas. That one act of charity changed how I viewed everything.

I have always thought of Christmas time, when it has come round, as a good time; a kind, forgiving, charitable time; the only time I know of, in the long calendar of the year, when men and women seem by one consent to open their shut-up hearts freely, and to think of people below them as if they really were fellow passengers to the grave, and not another race of creatures bound on other journeys.

Charles Dickens

CATHERINE HICKS

ACTRESS

For ten seasons, actress Catherine Hicks has played Annie Camden, a pastor's wife and beloved mother of seven on the WB's most popular television series, 7th Heaven. The program is now the longest running family drama in the history of television, surpassing perennial favorites Little House on the Prairie *and* The Waltons. *Hicks' resume includes an impressive array of projects in television, film, and theater (www.catherinehicksonline.com).*

I grew up in Scottsdale, Arizona when there was nothing there — no development, just the desert. At Christmastime, I used to ask my dad where the snow was, because the books I read always represented Christmas with illustrations of falling snow and pretty little streets lined with snow laden trees.

My father reminded me that Christ was born in a

desert just like ours. In reality, that's what Bethlehem was — a dry and dusty desert. I came to understand that he was right - my Christmas was actually more like what Mary and Joseph experienced when the baby Jesus was born than what my storybooks portrayed.

Our home was in the middle of a citrus grove. We had two grapefruit trees in our yard that I named Bambi and Sandi. Every Christmas, my dad climbed a ladder and together we strung lights on those two trees. Every year the trees grew taller and taller, so as my childhood drew to a close we had giant grapefruit trees full of lights. It was so beautiful.

When I reminisce about my childhood holidays now, I don't really remember the gifts as much as I do the traditions. My favorite custom was praying next to the manger. When I was a very young child, my mom found a wonderful rustic manger set at a store in Scottsdale. We filled that lowly wooden manger with straw each year; it probably looked much like what the holy family experienced on that first Christmas over two thousand years ago. At midnight on Christmas Eve we put the baby Jesus in the manger between Mary and Joseph and prayed as we looked over them. It was always a very sacred experience.

I've kept that humble manger all these years and have incorporated it into my own family traditions. It helps my husband and I maintain a spiritual focus on Christmas with our daughter. After all, Christmas isn't just about Santa, elves and reindeer; it's about the birth of our Savior. As it says in Luke 2:10-11: *I bring you good news of great joy that will be for all the people. Today in the town of David a Savior has been born to you; he is Christ the Lord (NIV).*

Away in a Manger

Away in a manger, no crib for a bed,
The little Lord Jesus laid down His sweet head;
The stars in the bright sky looked down where He lay,
The Little Lord Jesus asleep on the hay.

The cattle are lowing, the Baby awakes,
But little Lord Jesus, no crying He makes,
I love thee, Lord Jesus! Look down from the sky,
And stay by my cradle till morning is nigh.

Martin Luther

MIKE
JAMES

NBA PLAYER
(Photo: Toronto Raptors)

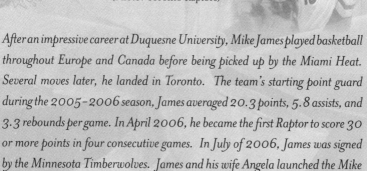

After an impressive career at Duquesne University, Mike James played basketball throughout Europe and Canada before being picked up by the Miami Heat. Several moves later, he landed in Toronto. The team's starting point guard during the 2005–2006 season, James averaged 20.3 points, 5.8 assists, and 3.3 rebounds per game. In April 2006, he became the first Raptor to score 30 or more points in four consecutive games. In July of 2006, James was signed by the Minnesota Timberwolves. James and his wife Angela launched the Mike James Scholarship Foundation in 2004 to help young people reach their full potential through education (www.mikejamesbasketball.com).

I grew up the youngest of seven children in Amityville, New York, which is on the south end of Long Island. My parents both worked really hard. Dad used to cook for a hospital, and Mom worked nights at a warehouse making hinges. She used to come home from work at 7:00

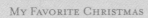

a.m. and then baby-sit all day to pay the bills. Then she'd fall into bed so she could be back at the warehouse by 10:00 p.m. There was never much extra money at our house.

My dad used to take me fishing with him, and I'll never forget one particular trip right around Christmastime. I'd been begging him for a new bike, so finally he said, "I'll make a deal with you: if you catch one fish, I'll buy you a bike this Christmas." The bet was on.

But no matter how hard I tried, I couldn't catch a fish to save my life. They just kept eating my worms! Finally, I caught one that was so little it was more like bait for the other fish. But in my mind, a fish was a fish so I showed it to my dad. He was like, "Man, that doesn't count!"

About a week before Christmas my dad sat me down and said, "Mike, you know it's been hard this year. I'm not going to be able to get the bike for you, I'm sorry." It hurt me so bad, but I understood. I fought back tears, but I understood... I'd been disappointed before.

When the night before Christmas came, there weren't many presents under the tree. But in the morning, there were toys and clothes and I was thankful that I had gifts to open.

After I opened the last package, my dad asked me to go out into the garage to get him something to drink. When I got out there I saw it... a red Piranha BMX bike with mag wheels and chrome pegs. It was like my own Bentley! I was so happy. I went outside and rode my new bike in the neighborhood with my buddies. Many of us got new bikes that year, so we were all out there jumping ramps together.

One of my boys didn't get a bike and asked me if I would let him ride mine and take it for a jump. I said, "No way, I will not let you ride my brand new bike that I just got." But he didn't give up, "Come on man, let me ride it!" I kept on saying no, but I finally gave in.

He jumped the ramp so high that he lost control and came down hard. The whole front rim was dented and he almost broke his arm. But I didn't care about that, I ran straight to my bike ... I was so mad at him! I couldn't ride it for a long time and it ended up with a different colored mag wheel on the front. So much for the Bentley!

It was a bittersweet Christmas. I was hurt about what happened to my bike, but I learned a very valuable lesson – material things are just material, easy come, easy go.

*Fail not to call to mind, in the course of the twenty-fifth of this month,
that the Divinest Heart that ever walked the earth was born on that day;
and then smile and enjoy yourselves for the rest of it; for mirth is
also of Heaven's making.*

Leigh Hunt

JERRY JENKINS

AUTHOR AND SPEAKER
(Photo: Jane McBee Photographics)

Author Jerry Jenkins has written more than 160 books, including the Left Behind *series which has sold more than 63,000,000 copies. His work has also appeared in dozens of periodicals, including* Time, Reader's Digest, Parade, *and* Guideposts. *Jenkins owns Jenkins Entertainment, a film-making company in Los Angeles and The Christian Writer's Guild, an organization devoted to educating, training, and supporting Christian writers (www.jerryjenkins.com).*

I love Christmas. I always have. I grew up in a close-knit family where Christmas was a time to remember, to reflect on the birth of Christ, and to epitomize the love and servant attitudes my parents and brothers and I knew we were to evidence throughout the year.

After one particular Christmas many years ago, my two older brothers and I — all elementary school kids — played with our new toys until we were tired of them ... three days or so. My mother brought an empty cardboard box into the dining room, sat us down, and told us of the kids at a local boys' orphanage who each got a piece of fruit, a candy bar, a comb, and a cheap toy in a standard package. "How about we give some of those guys a Christmas they won't forget?" Mom said. "Let's fill this box with toys that will make Christmas special. We'll do what Jesus would do."

One of my brothers had an idea. "With all my new stuff, I don't need all my old stuff!" He ran to get armloads of dingy, dilapidated toys, but when he returned, my mother's look stopped him.

"Is that what Jesus could do?"

He pursed his lips and shrugged. "You want us to give our new stuff?"

"It's just a suggestion."

"All of it?"

"I didn't have in mind all of it. Just what you think."

"I'll give this car," I said.

"If you don't want that," my brother said, "I'll take it."

"I'm not givin' it to you; I'm givin' it to the orphans."

"I'm done with this bow and arrow set," my older

brother said.

"I'll take that," I said.

"I'll trade you these pens for that model."

"No deal, but I'll take the pens and the cap gun."

We hardly noticed our mother leave the room. The box sat there, empty and glaring. We slipped away and played on the floor. But there was none of the usual laughing, arguing, rough-housing. Each played with his favorite toys with renewed vigor.

One by one we visited the kitchen. I found my mother at the table, her coat and hat and gloves on. Her face had that fighting tears look. No words were exchanged. She wasn't going to browbeat us into filling the box. Each of us returned to play quietly, as if in farewell to certain toys. And to selfishness.

A few minutes later, Mom came for the box. My oldest brother had put almost all his new toys in it. My next brother and I selected more carefully, but chose our best for the box. My mother never reported on the reception of the orphans, and we never asked. Years of childhood remained, but childishness had been dealt a blow.

Somehow, not only for Christmas but all the long year through,
The joy that you give to others
Is the joy that comes back to you.
And the more you spend in blessing
The poor and lonely and sad,
The more of Your heart's possessing
Returns to you glad.

John Greenleaf Whittier

LARRY
JONES

FOUNDER AND DIRECTOR OF
FEED THE CHILDREN

Larry Jones is the founder and president of Feed The Children, the nation's 3rd largest international charity based on private, non-governmental support. Feed The Children is a Christian non-profit relief organization that delivers food, medicine, clothing, and other necessities to people impacted by famine, war, poverty, or natural disaster. Last year, FTC shipped 183 million pounds of food and other essentials to children and families in all 50 states and around the world, supplementing more than 1,463,000 meals a day. Over the years, Jones has won numerous humanitarian awards for his tireless efforts (www.feedthechildren.org).

O**n December 7, 1988 at 11:41 a.m., a massive earthquake measuring 6.9 on the Richter Scale, hit the country of Armenia killing more than 25,000 people and leaving 500,000 homeless. Shortly after the disaster, Feed The Children had an opportunity**

to send a cargo plane filled with food and other relief supplies to the devastated region. There wasn't much time to prepare or react; I literally prayed and went.

Ordinarily I would take a cameraman and photographer along to chronicle the trip, but I was told there was only room for one person on the plane. I had to go alone. Yet the Lord opened door after door for me during that trip, it was an amazing thing to witness.

As I said, this was a cargo plane, so I got in the back of the aircraft, wrapped myself in a sleeping bag to stay warm and went to sleep. Our destination was the capital city of Yerevan, Armenia, approximately 47 miles from the epicenter of the quake in Spitak.

When we got word that Yerevan was fogged in, we were diverted to Constanta, an airport in Romania. They opened the airport just for us, so even though we didn't need it we refueled there. We nearly froze to death; the temperature was something like 30 degrees below zero, and all they had were little heaters about six inches across that did absolutely no good.

Eventually we made it to Yerevan. What a strange experience ... this was part of the Soviet Union, so it was a communist country. I didn't have a visa; there hadn't been time for that. Normally it would have been nearly impossible to enter the country without one, but when there's a natural disaster like an earthquake, you get by with things that you otherwise wouldn't.

I disembarked as they unloaded the supplies, and the plane turned around and left. I had absolutely no clue how or when I could get back home. I was taken to a monastery of the Russian Orthodox Church to stay for a few days. I had been up in the air for a total of three days and two nights and I was dead tired.

As I sat in the lobby waiting to be shown to my room, I thought I must have dozed off and was dreaming, because I saw Mother Teresa. I rubbed my eyes, shook my head and took another look just to be sure, but it was definitely her. I jumped up, grabbed my little pocket camera and asked another man to take a picture of us. There I stood with a Nobel Peace Prize winner, and one of the most famous humanitarians of our time, in a monastery in Armenia.

There was only one picture left on the camera, but we got it.

It was an amazing couple of days. I had four meals with Mother Teresa, once sitting on her right, once on her left and twice sitting across from her. She was extremely patient, fluent in numerous languages, and a very open person. Perhaps the best way to put it is that she was an ordinary person who had an extraordinary faith in God.

I went to two masses with Mother Teresa, even though I'm not Catholic. The first mass was at 6:00 a.m., and as we waited in the cold surrounded by ice and snow, she wore sandals with wool socks! We waited a long time for the chapel doors to open until somebody finally thought they'd better go check on the Father. Believe it or not, he was still in bed sleeping! But it was all worth it - in my wildest dreams I could have never imagined praying in an Armenian monastery chapel with Mother Teresa. I will always cherish that time.

For me to get what I needed, a photographer and videographer, I went down to the Yerevan Hotel, which was fondly nicknamed the "Watering Hole" because everybody met there at the end of the day. They were really high on tea and Turkish coffee, which to me is just like drinking grounds. At the hotel I met a man from ABC-TV France who worked their regional office. He told me they had a 50-passenger bus going up to Spitak with only five people on board and that he'd take me up there.

A photographer for *Time* magazine said to me, "If you'll get me on that bus with you, I'll take pictures and just give you the roll." So I got him and another woman, who was a stringer for *Life* magazine on board as well. An ABC videographer also offered his services — he said he would shoot some footage and give it to me.

So, there I was, on the other side of the world in a disaster with no journalistic resources whatsoever and suddenly I had a videographer and two award-winning photojournalists with me. Nobody but God Himself could have orchestrated a set of circumstances like that.

When we finally arrived in Spitak, I was speechless — there was complete and total devastation. The entire

city was destroyed. Because the earthquake had hit at noon, men were coming home to eat and women were in their homes preparing meals. That's why so many people were killed; they were home for lunch. Many children lost their lives because they were caught in unstable school buildings. If the quake had occurred even five minutes later, many of those young lives would have been spared.

When the ABC cameraman got through shooting his footage, he shot some for me. Then he made a special request... he handed the priest a branch and asked us to decorate it for Christmas. The Father and I found some Christmas ornaments at nearby apartment buildings and decorated that empty branch and stuck it in the ground. Then the cameraman shot it. There in the midst of the rubble sat a beacon of hope. It was a very poignant moment for all of us.

After spending four or five days in Armenia, I arrived home a few days before Christmas. On Christmas Eve, as I was sitting in my living room watching the ABC Evening News, Peter Jennings closed his newscast with the video of the Christmas branch that the Father and I had decorated just days before. It was very surreal — there I was sitting with my family in the living room of our comfortable home, but my heart was still in Armenia where I had seen unfathomable suffering. Over 25,000 people died as a result of the earthquake, thousands more were injured, and there were still people missing when I left.

One of the things that has really made a change in my life is to watch when the Lord finds someone in anguish and enters what I call their "circle of suffering." Whether they are hungry, whether they are thirsty, or whether they are spiritually in need, He enters their circle of suffering and ministers to them. That's what I'd just done in Armenia with the earthquake victims. I was honored to be allowed into their "circle of suffering."

As I sat in my living room on Christmas Eve and looked at that tree branch on television, I was overcome with emotion. Christmas is about family, Christmas is about the giving and receiving of gifts, and Christmas is about reaching out to those who are in need.

That particular Christmas, my gift to the people of Armenia was a planeload of food. But *my* Christmas gift was having the opportunity to spend time with Mother Teresa. It was an experience I'll never forget.

Voices in the Mist

The time draws near the birth of Christ:
The moon is hid; the night is still;
The Christmas bells from hill to hill
Answer each other in the mist.
Four voices of four hamlets round,
From far and near, on mead and moor,
Swell out and fail, as if a door
Were shut between me and the sound:
Each voice four changes on the wind,
That now dilate, and now decrease,
Peace and goodwill, goodwill and peace,
Peace and goodwill, to all mankind.

Alfred, Lord Tennyson

RACHAEL LAMPA

RECORDING ARTIST

At just 20 years old, Dove Award winning contemporary Christian recording artist Rachael Lampa has already recorded four albums. Her debut release, Live for You, *spawned four number one hits, including the award-winning song, "Blessed." Lampa has been featured in numerous publications including* USA Today, Seventeen, Teen People, Billboard, CCM. *Her greatest hits CD,* Blessed: The Best of Rachael Lampa *was released in the spring of 2006 (www.rachaellampa.com).*

I have a favorite tradition that we always do in my family. I have an older brother a younger brother and a younger sister and we're all really close. My brother and I live in Nashville now, but the rest of the family still lives in Colorado where I grew up. When we go back home we're all inseparable.

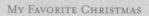
On Christmas Eve I'm usually singing at a service or something. It's always such a packed day that we end up being really tired by the end of the night. Usually we don't even eat our traditional Christmas Eve meal until around 9:00.

I say "traditional," but it's not your typical turkey or ham dinner. My dad is Filipino, so he fixes us this incredible ethnic food – egg rolls, rice and a Filipino chicken dish called Chicken Adobo. I look forward to that meal all day long. We pig out all night and then watch the movie *Home Alone*. We watch the same movie every year; in fact we try not to watch it the rest of the year so we can handle it!

After the movie is over we all cram into one room and have a slumber party. It was definitely a lot more comfortable when we were younger, but we still try to do it. It's a mess! We don't really sleep, but we act like it. Then of course we wake up and do Christmas; we read the Christmas story and open our presents from Santa.

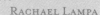

Our Christmas is all about sitting around and relaxing and just being home at the same time. There's no excuse for running to the computer and getting to work; it is quality time together celebrating our Savior's birth. So much of the year we're used to running and running and working and working, and so Christmastime is just really a time of rest for us. If you can make sitting around a tradition, then that's what it is!

Our hearts grow tender with childhood memories and love of kindred,
and we are better throughout the year for having, in spirit,
become a child again at Christmas–time.

Laura Ingalls Wilder

RUSS LEE

RECORDING ARTIST
(Photo: Stephen Kohl)

Singer/songwriter Russ Lee has been an integral part of two of Christian music's most beloved groups, NewSong and Truth. He has been featured on more than 10 #1 singles over the years, including "I Smile," which was one of the most played CCM songs of 2001. Altogether, Lee has been involved in 16 albums, including his latest solo recording, **Pictures on Mantels: The Best of Russ Lee,** *which was released in 2005 (www.russlee.com).*

I didn't grow up with a lot of things. From the time I was four years old, my mother was mentally ill and in and out of mental institutions. She had what would later be diagnosed as bipolar disorder. The chemical imbalance in her brain caused frightening mood swings. Some days she would be over the top happy and full of hope. Then without warning she would fade off into darkness. It was horrible, frankly. When my mom was with it, she was kind of like the Caucasian "Aunt Jemima." But when she wasn't with it, life was crazy and unpredictable.

Back in the middle to late 1960's, they would say people like my mom had "nerve problems." Doctors would prescribe drugs like lithium to dumb people down, figuring if they softened them to the point of being zombies they wouldn't hurt anybody or themselves. It was kind of a "feel good" therapy, but it robbed people like my mom of their quality of life.

Mom's illness made for a very dysfunctional home. Dad tried to be both mom and dad, but he just wasn't cut out for the nurturing part at all. He was a man's man... he was an outdoorsman, and had traveled the world with the navy. Playing "mom" was really hard on him.

We grew up feeling like our house was never quite a home. We also moved a few times because of financial problems. It was feast or famine in our household; my dad would sell our property so we'd have a little money and could breathe again. But then we would start buying things and all of a sudden we'd be right back in the same difficult situation. My childhood was up and down, back and forth and very confusing and difficult.

I remember one year when my brother and I thought for sure we weren't going to get anything for Christmas. We figured Santa Claus knew we'd been bad... probably because we were bad all the time! We were typical little boys; snakes and snails and puppy dog tails, that was us. We thought if we got anything — even something really small - it would be a miracle. Our dad told us he used to get things like new socks, oranges, and apples for Christmas and we'd be lucky if we even got that kind of stuff.

When I was eight years old my little brother and I were huge sports fans. We both told Santa we wanted Atlanta Falcons football uniforms; that's the page we had torn out of the Sears catalog. But we knew there was no chance we were going to get them. And being disappointed about that was going to prove once and for all that there was no Santa Claus.

But sure enough, we woke up on Christmas morning and found not only two complete Atlanta Falcons uniforms, but we also had a new football, a baseball glove and a bat. We scored big that year ... we hit the long ball!

My brother also got a Big Wheel — one with wheels that clicked - and I got my first guitar. Believe it or not my parents paid the same amount for the guitar that they did for the Big Wheel. So that tells you what kind of guitar it was! Still, it was my first guitar and started the whole love of music that eventually became my calling.

It was a massive Christmas, but at the same time it really messed me up. I was getting older and was starting to think there was no such thing as Santa Claus. But when I woke up Christmas morning to those amazing gifts, I was shocked. I knew my dad couldn't afford all of that. When my little brother said, "See, I told you there is a Santa Claus... there's no way Dad could have gotten this stuff," I knew he was right. And I've never doubted it again.

Now when my kids say, "Dad, come on, there's no Santa Claus," this is my response: "Yes there is, I know him personally. I know Santa Claus so well you wouldn't believe it ...!"

If…we open our hearts and embrace Him…not only to reap abundance and joy and health and happy fulfillment, but also for the cancellation of our sins — then this is the greatest welcome we can give to the Christ Child.

Norman Vincent Peale

KEVIN MAWAE

NFL PLAYER
(Photo: Tennessee Titans)

Center Kevin Mawae was signed by the Tennessee Titans in March of 2006 after playing four seasons with the Seattle Seahawks and eight with the New York Jets. A familiar face at the Pro Bowl, he has made six appearances at the game. Off the field, Mawae is known for his charitable contributions to the community. He serves as the spokesman for The David Center for Autism Research and is consistently involved in other fund-raising events for children.

When we were kids, my brother John and I were snoopers. About a week before Christmas one year, we found the 10-speed bikes our parents had bought us hidden down in the basement. So we really had to act surprised on Christmas morning, "Oh my gosh, look I got a new bike!" when down deep we'd known it for days.

There were four active, growing boys in our household, so you can image how much we used to eat. Every Christmas, my mom baked between 10-15 pies to keep us satisfied. She made each of our favorites: lemon meringue for my dad, pumpkin for one brother, and cheesecake for another. My favorite was pecan. So each of us had at least two pies set aside just for us.

My wife Tracy and I have started a new tradition with our own kids. Because Christmas is the celebration of Christ's birth, we make a birthday cake every year. And then on Christmas we all sing "Happy Birthday" to Jesus. The kids love it and truly understand that's the reason we celebrate the holiday ... it's not just about receiving gifts.

Another thing we do to maintain focus during the season is that Santa only brings our kids three presents each. Now they can get more gifts from aunts, uncles and grandparents, but they only get three big presents from us. Why three? Because that's what Jesus got from the wise men. After all, if it was good enough for Jesus, it better be good enough for them.

After Jesus was born in Bethlehem in Judea, during the time of
king Herod, Magi from the east came to Jerusalem and asked,
"Where is the One who has been born King of the Jews?"
On coming to the house, they saw the child with his mother Mary,
and they bowed down and worshiped him. Then they opened their
treasures and presented him with gifts of gold and of incense and myrrh.

Matthew 2: 1, 2, 11.

KEVIN MAX

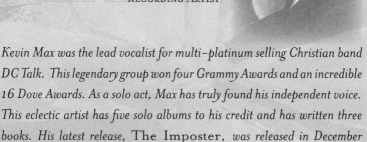

RECORDING ARTIST

Kevin Max was the lead vocalist for multi-platinum selling Christian band DC Talk. This legendary group won four Grammy Awards and an incredible 16 Dove Awards. As a solo act, Max has truly found his independent voice. This eclectic artist has five solo albums to his credit and has written three books. His latest release, The Imposter, *was released in December 2005 (www.kevinmax.com).*

I have so many great memories of Christmas. I grew up amidst the beautiful rolling hills surrounding Grand Rapids, Michigan. In this part of the state it snows quite a bit. We lived in a heavily forested area, and I can still picture the snow blanketing the tree branches after a storm. It looked just like a Currier & Ives postcard.

People loved coming out to our hobby farm for sleigh rides in the winter. My dad bought a couple of vintage,

Victorian sleighs at an Amish flea market to make the experience more authentic. He decorated the sleighs, cut a trail back in the woods and took people on trips throughout our extensive property. Dad is the biggest humanitarian person on the planet, and people came from everywhere for free sleigh rides. It was so picturesque, especially at Christmastime. There is something really special about a sleigh ride during the holidays.

When I was 12, our church decided to do a live nativity, and asked us if they could hold it at our house. It was pretty cool; we had a variety of "actors" dressed up in period costume to depict the birth the Jesus. And for this live nativity, they wanted me to play the part of Joseph. The Virgin Mary was played by a cute little round-faced, blonde Dutch girl in my Sunday School class named Connie.

At the time, we had a little palomino pony named Mike. Now, Mike was the most volatile of all the horses we'd ever owned. I mean, he had a serious Napoleon Bonaparte complex and didn't want anybody riding him. With our other horses, I could go out to the barn with my little brother and jump on their backs while they were eating. But I'd never dream of doing that with Mike.

Despite his shortcomings, Mike was the pony we used for the live nativity. Volunteers set up a camera and projector to film the holy couple as we rode Mike through the woods to "Bethlehem," which was really our barn. Inside the barn we had set up a little nativity scene complete with manger.

Mike was not at all happy that we were riding him. He kicked the whole time and actually kicked two or three different people on the "set." But that wasn't the only way he showed his displeasure — he was so angry that he defecated everywhere. And it was all caught on film! We have shots of Mike doing his business all the way from "Nazareth" to "Bethlehem." Not only was he mad because he was being ridden - I don't think he was too crazy about being filmed either.

It was all quite a production; we actually still have the projection slides of that whole experience. We watch it every once in a while, and it's so funny to see the clips of Mike and how angry he was. You could literally see anger on the face of that horse. It's a pretty cute Christmas memory!

Sing hey! Sing hey!
For Christmas Day;
Twine mistletoe and holly.
For a friendship glows
In winter snows,
And so let's all be jolly!

Author Unknown

BART
MILLARD

RECORDING ARTIST
(Photo: Mark Nicholas)

Bart Millard is the lead vocalist and front man for the successful multi-platinum selling Christian band, Mercy Me. In 2001 they released their debut album, Almost There, *and were instantly propelled into the spotlight with their smash hit,* I Can Only Imagine. *Mercy Me has already won five Dove Awards, including "Song of the Year," "Group of the Year," and "Artist of the Year." Millard also earned an individual Dove for Songwriter of the Year in 2002. Mercy Me has released five albums, including their latest,* Coming Up To Breathe, *which was released in the spring of 2006. Millard also recently released a solo project,* Hymned *(www.mercyme.com).*

My wife Shannon and I married on November 8, 1997. We had just gone full time with our music and it was an awkward place to be financially. It was one of those things; the music demanded all of our

time but it wasn't paying much. As a result, we were just barely getting by. I was making a whopping $11,000 a year, so needless to say our first Christmas was a little meager. But it was still one of the best times of my life.

We woke up on Christmas morning, turned on the Bing Crosby, sat in our home pants (pajamas for those who don't speak Bart and Shannonese,) and sipped the finest Swiss Miss hot chocolate around. Then we took turns opening our few gifts. After every gift, we posed for a photo with the goofiest face possible to express our excitement.

Even though that first Christmas together was sweet, I'd have to say my favorite Christmas memory of all time was the next year, the Christmas of 1998. We were still broke, but somehow I was able to give Shannon a huge surprise.

Over the previous few years I'd been able to save enough money to put a down payment on a new car. I was pretty sneaky... I bought the new car during the week and told Shannon that the car we traded in was in the shop and had to be left there. Then I made the trade, bought the new car and left it at my best friend's house for safekeeping until Christmas Day. In the middle of the night on Christmas Eve, he secretly drove it over and dropped it off at our house.

Shannon and I open gifts first thing in the morning and have always made the last gift the big one. I can't remember what I was pretending the big gift was, but I think it actually came across as a pretty lame Christmas. At the end of the gift exchange I said, "Oh yeah, there's one more thing." I don't recall exactly how I got her out to the garage, but she was still clueless when we got out there. I opened the garage door, and there was the new car with a big bow on it. She flipped out.

It was our first new car together, and it was pretty exciting considering we weren't living on much at the time. To surprise her with a new car in the driveway was pretty awesome. Honestly, I'm not very good at keeping secrets, so I don't know how I pulled it off.

Now that we have our kids, Sam, Gracie and Charlie,

Christmas has changed quite a bit. But I will never forget those first few years with just Shannon and me. The Christmas right before we started having kids, I think we realized something felt kind of empty. We wanted Christmas to be about somebody else instead of just us.

When Sam came along, everything changed and we started creating a whole new set of memories. Now from the day after Thanksgiving until New Year's Eve, we take a drive every night to look at Christmas lights, and try to find as many as we possibly can. That's been going on since Sam was born and he'll be the first one to remind us of it when Christmas comes around. It's become a great tradition.

Even though it can be a pain, my best memories of Christmases with the kids are ironically those long hours on Christmas Eve spent trying to put their dang toys together! Getting them to bed that night can be tough ... they always think they've seen Santa outside the window and it's a challenge to get them to stay asleep.

For Shannon and me, it used to be all about what

creative gifts were going to give each other — especially in those early days. Now as parents, the last thing we think about is whatever gift we're going to receive. It's all about the kids. And it's amazing!

I love the Christmas-tide, and yet,
I notice this, each year I live;
I always like the gifts I get,
But how I love the gifts I give!

Carolyn Wells

MARK
MILLER

RECORDING ARTIST

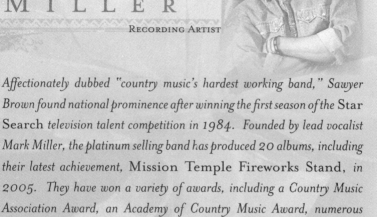

Affectionately dubbed "country music's hardest working band," Sawyer Brown found national prominence after winning the first season of the Star Search television talent competition in 1984. Founded by lead vocalist Mark Miller, the platinum selling band has produced 20 albums, including their latest achievement, Mission Temple Fireworks Stand, in 2005. They have won a variety of awards, including a Country Music Association Award, an Academy of Country Music Award, numerous TNN/Music City News Awards, and a trio of CMT Country Music Awards. After making music for more than 25 years and doing over 3,500 live shows, Sawyer Brown is still going strong (www.sawyerbrown.com).

O ur family used to have what you might call a "Walton Christmas," just like the TV show. I spent Christmas Day with my own immediate family, but on Christmas Eve, it was just a given that

everyone would go to my grandmother and grandfather's house in Ohio.

I had 21 first cousins and we spent every Christmas Eve together until I was in middle school. There was a 16-17 year age span amongst the cousins, so we all had somebody around our own age to play with. There was almost always snow, and we would sled, have snowball fights, make snowmen, and do all of those fun winter activities. The kids had so much fun playing together ... it was fantastic!

I also remember there being a tremendous amount of food. We would always eat first - the traditional turkey and dressing and ham - and then we would open gifts. It was all about the kids; I don't remember the parents ever even getting anything! Of course we had to draw names – with a group that size you'd have had to take out a small loan just to make it through Christmas.

When I was 12 my family moved to Florida, so getting together with the whole extended group became much more difficult. Christmas was never quite the same after that ... I missed the magic that happened when all of the cousins were together.

My favorite Christmas memories are filled with the sounds of children laughing, the love of family, and the wonder of a precious baby boy lying in a manger. He made the ultimate sacrifice for us so that we might celebrate.

Sweet Mary Cried

Written by Mark A. Miller and Gregg Hubbard
Travelin' Zoo Music (ASCAP) / Myrt & Chuck's Boy Music (ASCAP)

Mary, the Son of God is sleeping in your bed
It's a holy mighty crown that awaits His head
But that's not who sweet Mary sees at all
She sees a precious baby lying in a manger stall
Oh but He deserves more than this
This child who's know God's kiss

Chorus
And Mary, sweet Mary cries
And prays inside her heart for God to dry her eyes

And Mary, she understands That we're all in God's hands
Every mother, every child and sweet Mary cries

When the boy became a man they took Him away
He who was without sin was made to pay
When Mary looks upon the cross
She sees that precious baby lying in a manger stall
Oh but when she sees His face
Her heart can't help but break

Chorus

With all this celebrating we get lost along the way
When we forget the reason why we have a Christmas Day

And Mary, sweet Mary cries
And prays inside her heart for God to dry her eyes
And Mary, you understands
That we're all in God's hands
Every mother, every child and sweet Mary cries

*It was always said of him, that he knew how to keep Christmas well,
if any man alive possessed the knowledge. May that be truly said of us,
and all of us! And so, as Tiny Tim observed, God Bless Us, Every One!"*

Charles Dickens

NICOLE C. MULLEN

RECORDING ARTIST

An award winning singer, songwriter, and choreographer, Nicole C. Mullen is a dominant force in contemporary Christian music. She started out singing backup for Michael W. Smith and the Newsboys, wrote songs for Jaci Velasquez, and worked as a dancer/choreographer for Amy Grant. Now a hugely successful solo act, Mullen has 20 Grammy and Dove Award nominations to her credit (www.nicolecmullen.com).

My favorite part of the Christmas holiday is family. We have a lot of fun just being able to relax and enjoy each other, and also to enjoy what God has done in our lives.

As I think back about past Christmas seasons with my family, I'm reminded of a very special Christmas Day that came just over five or six years ago. My husband David and I, our daughter Jasmine, and my father went to visit

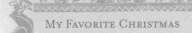

my grandfather who was living in a nursing home. My grandfather was suffering from Alzheimer's disease, and to be honest with you, the visit was a very difficult one.

When I walked in the nursing home I was immediately depressed; the stench of death was overwhelming. I remember thinking, "They have my papa here, the one who pastored people, the one who preached the Word in and out of season, the one who took in orphans and housed, clothed and fed them? The one who gave me a chance to sing from the time I was two."

My granddad had always been this robust, jolly, Santa Claus-sized man who was always laughing. I loved how he called me by my nickname, "Bubbles." When we arrived in his room, I witnessed something very different ... a frail old man confined to a wheelchair with his head drooped down. It broke my heart.

Sensing our discomfort, my dad took over and talked to Granddad as if he was still there and nothing had changed. My dad treated him with immense respect. "Hey there Dad, I brought you some gifts and your favorite thing!"

He then he reached into the bag he'd brought, pulled out some tangerines and peeled one for his father. Privately, I thought that was an odd thing to give as a Christmas gift. But then it really hit me. My grandfather didn't need a new tie or the latest gadget, but he'd always loved tangerines. It was the perfect gift after all.

When dad broke open the fruit, it was as if this fragrant smell of life directly contrasted the smell of death. I remember crying so hard that I had to leave the room. But then I realized that this was the same way Christ came into the world. He was a beacon of light against the stench and darkness of death. It was God in all His glory lying in a dirty manger with the reek of filth all around Him. And it was beautiful.

Great little One! whose all-embracing birth
Lifts Earth to Heaven, stoops Heaven to Earth.

Richard Crashaw

ANTHONY MUÑOZ

PRO FOOTBALL HALL OF FAME

Offensive tackle Anthony Muñoz was the Cincinnati Bengals' first-round pick of the 1980 NFL draft. Considered by many to be one of the best offensive tackles in history, Muñoz was elected to 11 straight Pro Bowls. He was the NFL Offensive Lineman of the Year in 1981, 1987, and 1988 and was inducted into the Pro Football Hall of Fame in 1998. Muñoz now devotes his time to impacting youth mentally, physically, and spiritually through the Anthony Muñoz Foundation (www.munozfoundation.org).

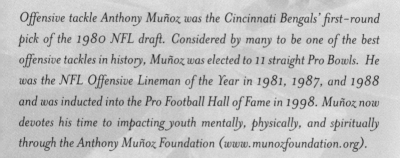

Even though my mom was a single parent and struggled to raise five kids on her own, she always had a Christmas tree, she always had the lights, and she always provided for us. Things weren't always that great, but every year we had presents under the tree.

Decorating the Christmas tree was something we all did together. I'll never forget the tinsel; we used it on

the tree along with the lights and it was beautiful. But we didn't like it so much *after* Christmas, when we had to remove that tinsel strand by strand, box it up and save it for the following year. As kids we weren't always crazy about the process; we had to be very careful removing each piece so it wouldn't snap. Still, it was a fun family thing we did and a really fond memory for me. I guess you could say we were the original recyclers!

One of the highlights of growing up in our house was Christmas Eve when my mom made homemade tamales, a traditional Hispanic Christmas delicacy. I don't know if we were more excited about staying up Christmas Eve waiting for Christmas Day to roll around and open presents, or about eating some homemade tamales.

Making tamales is very labor intensive; in fact, in Latin countries, making tamales is a social occasion where everybody pitches in. First Mom bought all the ingredients — things she couldn't always get at the average supermarket. She had to get the masa (corn meal), the corn husks and the meat, and then she made the chili.

The assembly is the tricky part. The first step is to put the corn husks back together to overlap them and hold the filling. Then you kind of smear the masa dough onto the husks like paste to hold it all together. Then you add the meat, fold them, roll them up, and at long last stack them in a special cooking can. Nowadays, of course, cooking implements have evolved, so modern day tamale makers can use steaming pans, but in those days she just used a large can. It was quite an art; she needed just the right touch to pack and stack the prepared talames into the can. To top it all off, we were really good eaters, so poor Mom had to make quite a few. Now looking back, I can really appreciate the sacrifice she made for us every year.

For my mom, Christmas was a financial stretch and it took saving and budgeting on her part to make it happen. Now as adults, we often sit back and think how amazing it was that she could provide Christmas at all understanding her financial hardships.

Now with children of my own, Christmas traditions have changed quite a bit. After all, it's kind of hard to duplicate the homemade tamales! Neither my wife nor I

come from spiritual backgrounds, so as children we didn't really look at the significance of Christmas — it was all about the presents. But as believers, we have made a conscious effort to bring Christ back into Christmas. We wanted to make sure that our kids understood the importance, first of all of our faith, and more importantly of why we're celebrating Christmas. It wasn't just about the number of gifts you received or their price tags… we were celebrating the birth of our Savior.

So while our two kids were growing up, the first thing we did after breakfast on Christmas morning was to gather around and read the Christmas story from the Bible. Doing that first helped us keep everything in perspective as to why we were celebrating Christmas.

Now, Christmas is so much more than bright, shiny tinsel — because we know that Jesus Christ is the light of the world.

We hear the beating of wings over Bethlehem and a light that is not of the sun or of the stars shines in the midnight sky. Let the beauty of the story take away all narrowness, all thought of formal creeds. Let it be remembered as a story that has happened again and again, to men of many different races, that has been expressed through many religions, that has been called by many different names. Time and space and language lay no limitations upon human brotherhood.

New York Times

LUIS PALAU

CHRISTIAN EVANGELIST AND AUTHOR
(Photo: Luis Palau Association)

Luis Palau is one of the world's most admired and respected Christian leaders. In four decades of ministry, he has preached the Gospel face to face to more than 21 million people. Now, using tools that are relevant to contemporary culture, Palau presents festivals around the world featuring recording artists from the pop, rock, and hip hop genres, along with action sports athletes and celebrities to reach huge audiences. He has written close to 50 books and his evangelistic messages can be heard daily on 2,100+ radio stations in 42 countries (www.palau.org).

In January, 1963, when my wife Pat was seven months pregnant, she surprised me with the announcement that it was time to go to the hospital. I was worried — she still had two months to go before she was full term.

After waiting in the hallway at the hospital for more than an hour, the doctor came up and told me there were

serious complications and suggested we pray. When he finally came out he looked more worried than before. "We're getting an incredibly strong heartbeat for only a seven-month fetus," he said, "and it is so irregular that I must tell you I'm not optimistic. I don't know how the baby is surviving with the heartbeat we're hearing." I kept praying.

Two hours later, the doctor found me in the waiting area once again. Only this time, he wore a huge grin. "Congratulations! You're the father of twin boys!" He had not been hearing one strong, irregular heartbeat at all, but two regular heartbeats! I'll never forget the day we brought Kevin and Keith home five weeks later. Their chances had been slim for a while, but they slowly became stronger and healthier.

Later that same year, we were commissioned to Costa Rica. We arrived just a few short days before Christmas. It was all very stressful; it was Pat's first Christmas outside the United States, it was following on the heels of John F. Kennedy's assassination and our twins weren't even a year old.

Knowing what we know now, we shouldn't have left the country when we did. But Pat had enrolled at the Spanish Language Institute and classes began the first of January. Pat cried her heart out on Christmas Eve. She had so many adjustments to make all at once — moving to a foreign land, being far away from her family and having our first Christmas with the boys.

Yet we have good memories of that Christmas, thanks to a super couple, David and Betty Constance, whom we met at language school. They had nearly completed their studies and were preparing to leave for ministry in my homeland of Argentina. Even though they were busy, they came over and we had a fun time together. It turned out to be a good Christmas after all.

Over the years, we have had many wonderful holidays. But one was particularly special. In the spring of 1980 we went to Scotland for a six-city tour. Just as we were leaving the country at the conclusion of the tour, Patricia and I found ourselves faced with the biggest challenge of our lives. She had discovered a lump in her breast and we rushed home to have a biopsy done.

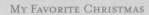

We sat in stunned silence when we heard the doctor's awful words, "The tumor is malignant and radical surgery must be performed immediately. We can't delay." Our worst fears had been realized ... Pat had cancer.

After we returned home that day, I headed down to my basement office. I needed a few moments alone to come to grips with this terrible blow. A hundred emotions welled up inside me and I began to weep. This was the sort of thing that happened to other people, not my Pat.

Suddenly my thoughts were interrupted by the strains of an old familiar hymn. Where was it coming from? Slowly it dawned on me that Pat was playing the piano and singing, "How Firm a Foundation." As the bottom was falling out of our lives, the Lord reminded us both how desperately we needed to base our security and strength in Him alone.

No one in this life is exempt from struggles, heartaches and difficulties. I'd known that since I was a boy and my mother was widowed at age 35. It was a miracle that she had been able to keep our family together after my dad died.

1980 was a challenging year. And because of Pat's ongoing battle with cancer and grueling chemotherapy treatments, I kept my travel schedule the following year to a minimum. One of the events was in San Diego, and it was our first full-scale English language, American crusade. I was delighted to have Pat join me. She spoke one morning to a group of 2,000 women about her struggles with cancer and the need to trust Jesus Christ to stand strong through life's storms. For 14 months I'd admired her strength and endurance despite repeated periods of weariness, sickness, discomfort and pain.

Our sons Kevin and Keith came home from college for Christmas a few days after a bone scan revealed Pat had no signs of cancer anywhere her body. That year we celebrated Christmas and New Year's in a big way! We were all back together again and for the moment, Pat's cancer was gone.

As a family, we thanked the Lord for sparing her life. In my heart, I also thanked God for using that time of adversity to give Pat a wider platform for her own ministry. As always, God's timing couldn't have been better.

Here is love, that
God sent His Son,
His Son who never offended,
His Son who was always
His delight.

John Bunyan

DEREK PARRA

OLYMPIC GOLD MEDALIST
(Photo: Bruce Gardner)

As an inline skater, Derek Parra reached the pinnacle of success. He won three national titles, two world championships, and 18 gold medals. In 1996, Parra traded in his wheels for ice skates to pursue his dream of competing in the Olympics. Soon after, the accolades started accumulating in speed skating as well. At the 2002 Olympic Games in Salt Lake City, Parra won a gold medal in 1,500 meters and silver in 3,000 meters (www.qsports.net).

Christmas can be a real challenge when you are a competitive speed skater. The U.S. team trials fall over the holiday season, so it can be next to impossible to get home for Christmas. If I was able to get home at all, it was only for a day or two.

My daughter Mia was born on December 14th, during the trials for the 2002 Olympic Games that were going to

be held in Salt Lake City. I received a phone call from my wife while I was at the trials that the baby was on the way. Hours later, I was on a plane and made it home just in time for the birth. The next day I headed back to Salt Lake City to solidify my spot on the U.S. team. After the trials were over, I was able to join my new family for our first Christmas together. What a special time that was.

The Olympic Games were an unbelievable experience for me. I gave up so much hoping for a moment like that, and when it actually happened it was just what I'd always dreamed of. There's no doubt in my mind that my daughter was one of my biggest inspirations.

She's four now. Her first few Christmases were all about playing with the bow and ripping up the boxes. That's all she wanted ... the gifts didn't seem to matter. When she was three she started grasping the whole concept of Christmas presents. When she received a toy she wanted, she opened it up and wanted to play with it right then. We had to do some serious negotiating to get her to open up something else. Opening up presents on Christmas morning was like a four hour ordeal because she wanted to play with each toy. The excitement within her was just a joy to watch.

The Christmas before the 2006 Olympics, Mia gave me a card with a little red Christmas ornament on it. I carried it with me in Italy — when I jogged, I heard it. When I was warming up skating, I heard it. I kept rubbing it here and there and thinking about my little girl. It meant the world to me.

Seeing Christmas through the eyes of my daughter has made the last four Christmases my most memorable ever. Christmas is exciting again ... I can't wait for the next one!

Christmas Eve was a night of song that wrapped itself about you like a shawl. But it warmed more than your body. It warmed your heart... filled it, too, with melody that would last forever.

Bess Streeter Aldrich

ANDY PETTITTE

MAJOR LEAGUE BASEBALL PLAYER
(Photo: Houston Astros)

Left hander Andy Pettitte made his major league debut in 1995 with the New York Yankees. Now a starting pitcher for the Houston Astros, he is a two-time American League All-Star. Pettitte has been part of six American League pennant-winning teams and four World Series championship teams.

My fondest childhood memories are of Christmases with my cousins at my grandmother's house. I was born in Baton Rouge, Louisiana and lived there until we moved to Texas when I was in fourth grade. Up until I was 10 or 11 years old, we spent every Christmas with the whole family.

On Christmas Eve we all went over to my grandmother's home — all the aunts, uncles and cousins. The Christmas tree was filled with hundreds of presents because there were so many grandchildren. There must have been 15 cousins, and when it came time to open presents we each found our own special corner in Grandma's tiny little house so we had some elbow room to rip them open.

The moms walked around passing out presents as we sat Indian-style waiting eagerly in our spots. Then my mom would announce, "On the count of three, dig in. One...two...three!" It was complete pandemonium. As we were opening our gifts, the dads walked around and collected the spent wrapping paper to maintain some semblance of order. Because it was such a free-for-all, we accidentally lost a lot of presents to those garbage bags. Sadly, we probably lost half the presents we opened — or at least critical pieces of them!

After the presents were all opened, the cousins sat together and watched old animated Christmas classics like *Rudolph the Red-Nosed Reindeer* and *Frosty the Snowman*. We did the exact same thing every year, and no matter how many times we saw those movies, we watched them like it was the very first time.

Now my wife and I are trying to make memories for our own children. This past Christmas was particularly significant for me because we had our last child in May. Obviously, we don't know exactly what's going to happen, and there's always a chance God could bless us with another baby, but we feel like our family is finally complete. So for the first time, we celebrated Christmas with all four children.

In Proverbs 22:6 it is written: *Train a child in the way he should go, and when he is old he will not turn from it.* (NIV) So, on Christmas Eve we always try to read the Christmas story out of the Bible. My wife's family did that when she was growing up, so we've incorporated it into our family traditions as well. Now our two oldest boys are able to read out loud, and it is such a joy to hear them retell the wondrous story of the baby Jesus.

The only real blind person at Christmas-time
is he who has not Christmas in his heart.

Helen Keller

RICKY SKAGGS

RECORDING ARTIST
(Photo: Erick Anderson)

Ricky Skaggs is a country and bluegrass music superstar. All told, Skaggs has 11 Grammy Awards, a Dove Award, 8 Country Music Association (CMA) Awards, 8 Academy of Country Music (ACM) Awards, 8 TNN Music City News Awards, and 9 International Bluegrass Music Association (IBMA) awards. In 2003, he was included on CMT's list of the "40 Greatest Men of Country Music." Together with his wife Sharon and their kids, they perform live holiday shows and have produced a holiday recording called A Skaggs Family Christmas — Volume I *(www.skaggsfamilyrecords.com).*

I've got a lot of wonderful Christmas memories from my own childhood and from when my kids were little. Recently, my wife Sharon and I were cleaning out our garage, going through boxes and trying to get things organized and put away. We hadn't seen the contents of some of these boxes for nearly five years, so it was fun to run through old pictures and memorabilia. For us, Christmas has always meant family.

All those memories are great but I've got to say, in all honesty, that my favorite Christmases are the ones we do together now for our Skaggs Family Christmas shows. When our kids were growing up and we celebrated with my parents, Christmas was just a one or two day event. But Skaggs Family Christmas shows are different. For the last three years we have put on live shows to celebrate the season — and the celebration lasts for pretty much the whole month of December. Because we start before Thanksgiving weekend, we get into the Christmas spirit right off the bat.

It's been an incredible experience for my wife and me to watch our two youngest kids share their talents and gifts with the whole world. It's wonderful to hear them talk on stage about what Christmas means to them and to share their memories of Christmases here in Tennessee.

Probably the most memorable Skaggs Family Christmas was our very first show at the Myerson Center in Dallas,

RICKY SKAGGS

Texas. I had just found out that day that I had been nominated for six Grammy awards, so that was pretty big news. And I thought to myself, man, what can top that?

After the show began, I introduced our daughter Molly. When she went out and sat at the piano, I marveled at the comfort she had talking to the audience. Her mother and I sat off stage, and held hands as our little girl, all grown up and full of confidence, sat out there doing what she loves to do. We'd never really tried to push her, but instead encouraged her and tried to give her the tools she needed to do what she wanted to do. So it was great to see her shine.

She wasn't afraid at all; she was just herself and really related to the audience. She knocked that performance right out of the ballpark! And then to see the reaction of the crowd... they weren't applauding for me and Sharon, they weren't applauding for the Skaggs and the Whites; they were applauding for Molly.

That was just the biggest shock and biggest surprise for me — I guess it wasn't really a surprise, because I knew she

had the talent to garner that kind of applause, but it was the newness of seeing one of my children applauded for her own talent and hard work. For the first time, I had to look at her as Molly Skaggs the performer, not just Molly Skaggs my little girl.

It was a bitter-sweet thing to tell you the truth; sweet in the sense that I was glad to see her achieve that for herself, but it was also a little tough letting go of the little girl and watching her pass into adulthood as a musician and an entertainer. It's great to see our kids moving out and doing their own thing now — we're so proud of all of them.

No question, these Christmases are the most memorable because we're making memories that will last a lifetime. These are the times we will always look back on and always cherish.

Oh! lovely voices of the sky
Which hymned the Saviour's birth,
Are ye not singing still on high,
Ye that sang, "Peace on earth"?

Felicia Hemans

BRANDON SLAY

OLYMPIC GOLD MEDALIST

Brandon Slay won the Olympic Gold Medal for Freestyle Wrestling at the 2000 Games in Sydney, Australia. Since the Olympics, he has operated an organization called Greater Gold, which prepares young people to reach their full academic and athletic potential while planting seeds of Biblical truth. Slay travels across the nation conducting wrestling clinics, speaking to youth groups, churches, schools, and corporations (www.brandonslay.com).

W hen I was ten years old, all I wanted for Christmas was a Dingo. Not the wild dog from Australia, but a go-kart. Now this wasn't your ordinary go-kart; it had big black rear tires with gold rims on them... it was really cool. It was actually more like an all terrain vehicle than a go-kart. My best friend Brandon Brown had one and even though he let me drive his all the time, I wanted one of my own. Sadly, I knew there was

little chance I would ever get one.

That year, my dad and I went over to Brandon's house and spent Christmas morning with his family. When we went out to the garage, I saw the most awesome, brand-new Dingo parked inside. I was so jealous — I knew Brandon's dad, Bob, had bought one for himself. I remember saying "Bob, that's nice, you got one too?" And they all started laughing — and I had no clue why.

Bob just kind of smiled at me and said, "Do you like it?" "Like it? No, I love it. I wish I could have one of those!" I answered. They told me to sit down in it, start it up and take it for a spin. When I came back to the house, I was totally taken aback when my dad told me it was mine! I thought he was kidding and told him to knock it off and quit teasing me. But when my dad saw how excited I was he started to cry and I knew it was true. I'll never forget that moment...

Little boys love getting wild, and are notorious for wanting to drive anything on wheels and wreck as much stuff as possible. For me, having this ATV meant I could drive around in the dirt and bump into things... in other words be a rough and tumble little boy.

For the next month, I was on that thing non-stop — you couldn't get me off of it. Brandon and I drove our Dingos all over the place; to our friends' houses, and tooling around the country side, through fields and ditches. There were a lot of ranches out where we lived and we were surrounded by horses and cattle and chickens. One of my favorite memories of riding my Dingo was going to "The Country Store." We drove our vehicles up to the door, parked and went inside and got ourselves a large, cold drink to cool us off in the blazing West Texas sunshine. It was a great place to spend my childhood.

Thinking back on it now, the whole experience reminds me of the Orson Wells film, *Citizen Kane.* My Dingo reminded me in some ways of "Rosebud," the name of the sled from Kane's childhood. At the very end of the movie you finally realize that the only joy this man had experienced in his life had been when he was a 10-year-old little boy going down the hill on "Rosebud." Nothing

after that fulfilled him to the same degree. It was really heartbreaking.

If I didn't have Christ in my life, who knows, I might just be sitting here thinking I wish I could go back to when I was ten years old riding that Dingo. But I know true joy — true joy comes from having a relationship with our Savior.

Let Christmas not become a thing
Merely of merchant's trafficking,
Of tinsel, bell and holly wreath
And surface pleasure, but beneath
The childish glamour, let us find
Nourishment for soul and mind.
Let us follow kinder ways
Through our teeming human maze,
And help the age of peace to come
From a Dreamer's martyrdom.

Madeline Morse

GARY SMALLEY

AUTHOR AND SPEAKER

One of the country's foremost authors and speakers on family relationships, Dr. Gary Smalley has written and co-written 28 best-selling books, including his 2006 release, The Two Sides of Love, *which he co-wrote with John Trent. All combined, he has sold an incredible six million books in addition to millions of supplemental videos. His work has garnered him an Angel Award and two Gold Medallion Awards for excellence in Evangelical Christian literature. Smalley has been seen on numerous national programs including* Oprah, Larry King Live, *and* The Today Show *(www.graysmalley.com).*

When I was a young child, I can remember being very, very poor. I was the youngest of five children and we all lived in a small rental place in Downey California. My father often worked out of state as a merchant marine, and my mother put in long hours

in the kitchen of a restaurant. It was war time, so money was very tight. Because our parents were gone much of the time, my brothers and sisters usually took care of me.

The Christmas of 1945, when I was five years old, I remember my mother telling us there wasn't enough money for any gifts. But she would cook a great Christmas dinner and we could have a family time together. I can remember comparing myself with my friends who told me how many gifts they had under the Christmas tree. I'm not sure we even had a Christmas tree that year. I was really, really sad.

When Christmas morning arrived, we had an unexpected knock at the door. There stood my aunt Gladys, my father's sister. I didn't know her at all, but I knew *about* her. She was sort of upper class and snobbish and worked at

(Marianne, 9 and Gary, 4)

an upscale department store in downtown Long Beach, California. My father's family was very wealthy, but had disowned him when he married my mother who came from the wrong side of the fence. My parents had been struggling to make ends meet ever since.

Needless to say we were surprised to see her standing at our front door. She had gotten up early and driven 40 or 50 miles so she could be there on Christmas morning. When my mother opened the door my aunt said, "Are you having a great Christmas?" Everybody answered, "Sure," but we were all really sad. Then she said, "If Santa missed you, I think he got confused and went to my house by mistake. Why don't you guys come out to my car?"

So we all walked out to the driveway, but we had no idea what she was talking about. When we got to her car, we all just screamed — her car was literally filled with Christmas gifts! She'd even put names on the packages so we brought them into our home and opened them up.

Somehow she had known about the struggles our family was going through, and really came through for us that Christmas of 1945. It was the most unbelievable experience and one I'll never forget.

It is the one season of the year when we can lay aside all gnawing worry,
indulge in sentiment without censure, assume the carefree faith of
childhood, and just plain "have fun." Whether they call it Yuletide, Noel,
Weinachten, or Christmas, people around the earth thirst for
its refreshment as the desert traveller for the oasis.

D.D. Monroe

CHARLOTTE SMITH

WNBA PLAYER
(Photo: Mitchell Layton)

Now on the roster for the Indiana Fever, 6' forward Charlotte Smith is a seven-year veteran of the WNBA. In 2004, she led the WNBA in 3-point field goal percentage and on July 15, 2004 she recorded her 1,000th career point. In her youth, Smith was awarded a full scholarship to the University of North Carolina at Chapel Hill. The most decorated player in the history of UNC's basketball program, she is the only woman to have her jersey retired. In the off season, Smith is on the coaching staff for the UNC women's basketball team.

My favorite Christmas moment was just this past Christmas. It's on the top of my list partly because it was the first Christmas I had at my new home in Chapel Hill, but more importantly, because I was able to spend it with my dad.

Five years ago my dad was diagnosed with cancer. It

started in his prostate, but by the time the doctor's found it, it had metastasized to his bones. The cancer was so advanced that they only gave him a year to live. According to the oncologists, he should have been gone a long time ago, but he's still here!

We all attribute dad's longevity to his unwavering faith. Not only does his faith help him get by day to day, but it encourages and strengthens me too. When I'm dealing with the minor issues of daily living, I look at how he handles his life-threatening illness. It's amazing to see how his faith has never faltered.

It reminds me of the book of Job in the Bible. Job went through so much; his whole family was killed, he lost all of his servants and livestock, and he was stricken with excruciating boils over his entire body, yet he didn't denounce God.

My dad is kind of the same way. It amazes me how he has the strength to make it through each day. He has endured so much pain over the last few years that I know there have been times when heaven sounded like a better option. But he feels like he has so much Kingdom work to do for Christ here on Earth that he continues to stay strong.

So this Christmas, I realized what a huge blessing it is that my dad is still alive. Sometimes we all get so caught up in the perspective of gifts as far as Christmas is concerned that we forget to just be thankful for the little things. And the thing I am most thankful for is life itself. Even though my dad wasn't feeling well this Christmas, it was great to have him around.

(Photo: Mitchell Layton)

Love is what's in the room with you at Christmas
if you stop opening presents and listen.

Author unknown

TODD
SMITH

RECORDING ARTIST

Todd Smith is one-third of the critically acclaimed ensemble **Selah.** *Formed in 1999, the trio has released a staggering six albums, including their latest recording,* **Bless the Broken Road — The Duets Album,** *which was released in August 2006. Like most of their CDs, the latest one features an African themed song, inspired by Smith's upbringing in Congo. The group has combined sales of more than one million units and has won four coveted Dove Awards, most recently the "2005 Inspirational Album of the Year" (www.selahonline.com).*

One cold winter evening when I was about four years old, my mom, sisters and I were sitting down in the living room watching the popular series, *The Waltons* on television. When my mom smelled something burning, she went into the utility room where the heater was located to check out the smell. It was a

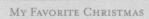

kerosene heater, and to my mother's horror, the unit was on fire. As she hustled us all out of the house to safety, the furnace exploded, setting everything in that room on fire. In no time the wind carried the flames throughout the rest of the house, and the entire wooden structure was rapidly engulfed.

Because we were so far out in the country, two different fire departments argued for nearly 15 minutes as to who was going to have to come out and help us. One of them finally came, but they quickly ran out of water and had to use our pond. In the end it was too little, too late and our home burned to the ground.

I suppose this seems out of place in a book of favorite Christmas memories, but that one experience triggered a chain of events that would ultimately change my destiny. Three days after the fire, my dad, a traveling evangelist and singer who was performing in California, still couldn't reach us and didn't know why. My aunt finally contacted him and told him that there had been a fire and we'd lost everything. When he found out we were all safe, he got down on his knees and thanked God that he wasn't going home to four funerals. In his truck on the way home, my dad felt as if God were sitting in the seat right next to him calling him to go to Africa and become a missionary. Life would never be the same.

My father grew up in the Belgian Congo (now the Democratic Republic of Congo) as the son of missionaries. So the idea of going to Africa didn't seem that far-fetched to him. But to my mother — well, that was another story. She never wanted to go to Africa. When my dad told her that he thought the Lord was calling us to Congo, it was undoubtedly the furthest thing from her mind. "The house is still smoldering and you want to go to Congo?" she said to him.

The following October we moved to Africa. I was only five years old when we arrived there and I was in serious culture shock; it was hot, it smelled, there was no good food, and even though my parents had stayed there before, the hotel we were in had definitely seen better days.

One Sunday after our arrival, we went to the American church for a worship service. The custom at this church was for newcomers to stand up, introduce themselves and tell everyone what they were doing in Congo. My dad got up and said, "I'm Jim Smith and I'm here with my family. We will be going out to a mission station in Nkara."

After the service, this wonderful lady named Judy Volth came up to my mother and introduced herself. She told us her husband worked at the American Embassy and they had a membership to a private Portuguese club with a swimming pool. My mom was thrilled when Judy asked if we would all like to go with her to the club — but not nearly as thrilled as we were!

When Judy came to pick us up, she took one look at the hotel we were staying in and told us to pack our bags. It was really that bad. She loaded us up and that same day we moved into her house. We stayed with them for three months; I can't imagine what kind of a sacrifice that was on their part. They basically took us in as family; when I think about it now, it almost brings tears to my eyes that they did that without even knowing us.

One of the best parts of living with them was that they

had commissary privileges at the large American Embassy. In other words, we got American food... which for a missionary kid, was a very big deal. Our diet up to that point had consisted of more "local" fare; certainly not hamburgers and hot dogs.

The Volth's had a big beautiful house with air conditioning and fans, which was a welcome respite in the steamy Congo climate. They also had a couple of kids. We celebrated our first African Christmas with them and had a wonderful time.

After about three months as spoiled houseguests, we moved to Nkara, which is about 300-400 miles out in the bush. Before we had left Michigan for Africa, my parents had packed about 30 large barrels worth of supplies for our new home. The barrels contained both household things and clothing; my mom had to plan for three years in advance for things like clothing sizes, birthday and Christmas presents. Whatever we might need in the future, she had to anticipate before we left American soil.

Unfortunately, we didn't get those barrels for a very

long time. My parents had accidentally packed the bill of lading inside one of the barrels rather than keeping it with them. In other words, the permission we needed to take possession of our belongings was inaccessible. Congolese government officials wanted to be paid off before we could get our stuff, and my dad just wouldn't do it.

(Photo: back (l-r): Shawn, Nancy and Jim Smith; front (l-r): Todd, Jack and Nicol Smith)

So when it came time for our first Christmas at the mission station, we didn't have any of our belongings. My grandfather had built a house when he was stationed there, so at least we had a place to live. But we had no Christmas tree — not even a fake tree — and there aren't too many pine trees in the African bush.

But that didn't stop us. We got a tin bucket, filled it with dirt and deposited some palm fronds we had cut from one of the trees in our back yard. I have no idea how we got it, but somehow we had popcorn, and strung it around our "tree" to make it a little more festive.

There were no gifts under the tree that year. Instead, we all drew pictures for each other; for my parents I drew my hand on a piece of paper. I remember telling my mom, "Mommy, I don't have much, but I love you with all my heart." That was her gift. My sister gave me dental floss; I think she was trying to tell me something.

We had mango trees in our yard, so instead of apple pie, Mom made mango pie. But beyond that, we didn't have much of a traditional Christmas dinner. Because our location was so remote, we had to order supplies from South Africa, and a lot of times our shipments didn't come for months. We just didn't get anything in time for Christmas.

Even though we had nothing to give, and our celebration didn't possess any of the normal trappings of the holidays, it's interesting that I remember that Christmas more fondly than any of the other ones we had in Africa. Looking back on it now, that Christmas was special because we just *were*... there wasn't a lot of ceremony

and commercialism, we were just together. I learned that year that Christmas isn't about the gifts or decorations, it's about being together. And that's a lesson I've never forgotten.

Best of all, Christmas means a spirit of love, a time when the love of God and the love of our fellow men should prevail over all hatred and bitterness, a time when our thoughts and deeds and the spirit of our lives manifest the presence of God.

George F. McDougall

JOHN
SMOLTZ

MAJOR LEAGUE BASEBALL PLAYER
(Photo: Atlanta National
League Baseball Club)

A dominant force in the major leagues since his debut in 1988, pitcher John Smoltz has made a significant impact on America's favorite pastime. In 1996, the seven-time All-Star won the Cy Young Award, leading the National League in wins (24), winning percentage (.750), innings pitched (253 2/3), and strikeouts (276). Known for his faith and philanthropic spirit, Smoltz was chosen by his peers as the Major League Baseball Players Association's "Marvin Miller Man of the Year" in both 2002 and 2003. In 2005, he was the recipient of the Roberto Clemente Award, an annual honor that recognizes the player who best exemplifies the game of baseball, sportsmanship, and community involvement (www.johnsmoltz.org).

O ne Christmas when I was about nine years old, my parents took my brother, sister and I on a motor home trip from our home in central Michigan to the picturesque Upper Peninsula. There was

so much snow that year you wouldn't have believed it. The roads were still good enough to get the RV up there, but once we arrived at our campsite there was an incredible snowstorm. Fortunately, we'd towed a Jeep behind the camper so we were still able to get around.

We went with another family so there was a bunch of kids, and for several days we just played in the snow and hung out together. We slept in the motor home, but did everything else outside. All of the cooking was done out on the campfire … we really roughed it. What an experience that was!

We flew all over the place and had a great time doing it! There was so much snow that we hooked up two toboggans to the Jeep and took turns getting rides — boys on one end and girls on the other. I can still see it in my mind's eye — the Jeep was probably pulling us at 30-35 miles an hour, so all it took was a gentle nudge and the toboggans would roll.

I remember my fingers and toes being so cold that I was actually crying. I'm sure we all had borderline frostbite, but we were having so much fun we didn't want it to end. Waiting for my appendages to thaw out was one of the worst feelings in the world, but it was a blast and a memory I will never forget.

Years later, after I had kids of my own, I thought it would be fun to take them on a road trip too. Only this time we drove from our home in Georgia all the way up to Michigan to visit my parents for Christmas. My wife and I had two very young children at the time, and people thought I was crazy for doing it. We got a 27' motor home, loaded it with kids and presents and hit the road.

On the way up, we got hit with a nasty ice storm outside Indianapolis and had to stop. Ironically, when we got up to Michigan it was bone dry and stayed that way the whole week we were there. It never snowed and there was nothing on the ground; we were bummed out because we wanted the kids to see snow. But we did all the family stuff and had a wonderful time nonetheless.

On the way home, we hit Ohio and the bad weather started. It was one of those massive snowstorms — the farther south I drove the worse it got. When we got to Nashville, Tennessee, we stopped at a gas station to wait it out. But the attendant told me if I stopped there I'd be stranded for a week. There was already 4"-6" of snow on the ground, and Tennessee natives weren't used to driving in those conditions.

The motor home wasn't exactly built for winter driving; the drive through the Smokey Mountains was nothing short of harrowing. I recall trucks passing us and the fear I felt as I tried to keep our vehicle on the road.

When we finally made it home, I woke up every half hour and saw headlights … the drive had been that tense. In fact, for a week my forearms ached from gripping the steering wheel so tightly – I hadn't realized I'd been white-knuckling it to make it home safely. If my goal had been to make memories, it was an unqualified success.

Now that I'm a Christian, I have mixed feelings about Christmas. People have commercialized the holiday to the point that there is far too much pressure and stress. I hate it; I hate that somebody has to feel pressure to give

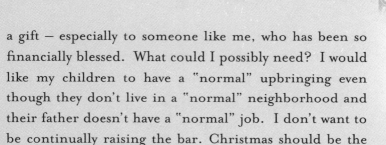

a gift — especially to someone like me, who has been so financially blessed. What could I possibly need? I would like my children to have a "normal" upbringing even though they don't live in a "normal" neighborhood and their father doesn't have a "normal" job. I don't want to be continually raising the bar. Christmas should be the day we celebrate the birth of Christ by spending time with family, not by giving gifts to each another.

As far as my family is concerned, I'm probably viewed more as a "bah humbug" than anything else. In my own defense, I'm trying to teach Godly principles rather than the traditions of the world. Too often, people forget that Christmas should be centered on Christ.

The greatest joy I have is blessing other people, whether I'm serving those less fortunate or simply bringing notoriety to Christ. I struggle with the "give me, give me, more, more, let me open up more presents" attitude. It has bothered me so much, in fact, that a couple of years ago I decided to make a bold statement. It didn't go over real well, but I told our kids they wouldn't be getting any presents that year... not from their parents or grandparents. In lieu of those gifts, we took their monetary value and made a donation to King's Ridge Christian School, the school they attend.

I'll admit that nobody was very happy with me, including my mom and dad, but even though it wasn't a very popular decision, it was a tremendous blessing to my kids. It taught them a couple of lessons: first of all, it was eye opening because they had no idea how much money people really spent on them. And more importantly, when the school recognized them for their gifts, they learned what a great feeling it is to give back. Now we make a habit of serving others at Christmastime by bringing toys to shelters and hospitals. The joy we experience from that can't be bought at any price.

(Photo: Atlanta National League Baseball Club)

186

When Christmas is over

We've put away the ornaments,
And burned the Christmas tree;
The Christmas fun is over — but
The Christ Child, where is He?

He lives in gifts and toys we share
With children who have few
And in the acts of kindness
We do the whole year through.

Corinna Marsh

KIMIKO
SOLDATI

OLYMPIC ATHLETE
(Photo: Tony Duffy)

Kimiko Soldati was honored to represent the United States of America in the 2004 Olympic Games in Athens, Greece. A highly decorated diver, she was the NCAA 1-Meter Champion in 1996; 2001 and 2002 U.S. Diver of the Year; 2001 and 2002 U.S. National Champion; 2002 World Cup Silver Medalist; 2001 Goodwill Games Bronze Medalist, and a 2004 American Cup Champion. She now focuses her time and energy raising her baby boy and doing motivational speaking (www.kimiko-usa.com).

When I think about Christmas, I think of my mom. When I was in fourth grade my mom was diagnosed with breast cancer. After a period of remission, the cancer returned, but this time it had moved into her bones. So for much of my childhood, my mother was very sick and in a great deal of pain. She eventually succumbed to the disease when I was in high school.

Christmas is wonderful, but it can also be a hard time of year for people who've experienced loss. Because of that, I try to focus on the many fond memories I have before cancer impacted our family.

Music was always a big part of the holiday for us. For many years, my brother and I played Christmas carols; I played the violin and he played the piano. We got to the point where we weren't really playing those instruments anymore, but we still busted them out each Christmas and tried to play carols for the family.

One of the other things we tried to do every year was build a snowman. I grew up in Colorado, so if the weather cooperated, our goal was to build the biggest snowman we could. It was often so huge that we had to use a tall ladder to finish it off.

My mom was really big into family, so for Christmas we either had family at our house or we traveled to the home of a relative. When you're a kid, it's all about the presents and the fun. Yet when I look back at it now, I realize it wasn't just about that for me – it was about family. I can credit my mom for that.

One of my most treasured possessions is a video we taped the Christmas when I was ten years old... coincidentally right about the time my mom found out she had cancer. It was when video cameras first came out, and I remember ours being big and bulky, totally unlike the compact cameras we have today. In the video, you can hear the Andy Williams Christmas album playing in the background with me hamming it up lip synching to the music. We played that record over and over every year, it was like a tradition.

That videotape is one of my favorite things to watch. It brings tears to my eyes because I miss her so much, but it's neat to see my mother so vibrant and alive. Sadly, many of my childhood memories are of my mom's illness, so I love having this memento to remind me of the good

times as well.

Even though my husband Adam never got to meet Mom, he can watch that videotape and see her, hear her talk and hear her laugh and get a sense of who she was. And she was a wonderful woman.

Christmas – that magic blanket that wraps itself about us,
that something so intangible that it is like a fragrance.
It may weave a spell of nostalgia. Christmas may be a day of feasting,
or of prayer, but always it will be a day of remembrance –
a day in which we think of everything we have ever loved.

Augusta E. Rundel

NANCY
STAFFORD

ACTRESS, AUTHOR AND SPEAKER
(Photo: Russell Baer)

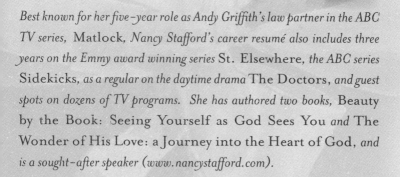

Best known for her five-year role as Andy Griffith's law partner in the ABC TV series, Matlock, *Nancy Stafford's career resumé also includes three years on the Emmy award winning series* St. Elsewhere, *the ABC series* Sidekicks, *as a regular on the daytime drama* The Doctors, *and guest spots on dozens of TV programs. She has authored two books,* Beauty by the Book: Seeing Yourself as God Sees You *and* The Wonder of His Love: a Journey into the Heart of God, *and is a sought-after speaker (www.nancystafford.com).*

E ight years ago, my husband Larry and I bought a small ranch in southern California. Rancho Monte Nido ("Mountain Nest Ranch") is a place of refuge, seclusion and beauty, and we make it available as a retreat center for people who need healing and restoration. It's the perfect place to dial down and get back to the heartbeat of God.

Larry and I spend so much time building and maintaining the ranch and living our crazy lives, we find that sometimes *we* also desperately need a place of refuge. One of the things we absolutely try to do every year is spend our Christmas at the ranch.

We don't have any immediate family in California; Larry's family is scattered and his parents have passed away, and my family is all in Florida. Plus, our daughter and grandson are in Texas. So, our adopted family, made up of four of our God kids and their sweet, precious parents, another single friend and a variety of special people, descend on the ranch at Christmas time each year.

Some of my most cherished adult memories are of Christmases at the ranch. If we're fortunate enough to have snow, we start a fire in the wood burning stove, throw

CDs on the stereo, light candles all throughout the house and eat way too much food. There's always something baking in the oven and a pot of mulled cider simmering on the stove. The aroma is absolutely heavenly.

The children are all over the place, of course — it's a fun getaway for them. If there's snow, the parents bring up little sleds or we just improvise and stick the kids in garbage can lids and they sled down the hill. Sometimes the young boys bring up bb guns and do target practice. Whatever the activity, they have a ball!

For the adults, it's all about relaxation. On Christmas Day, we eat for a while and then people wander off — they might hike the trails or simply catch a luxurious nap in one of the cottages. Being at the ranch forces everybody to stop for a while and get out of the cycle of their busy lives. And we get a chance to catch up with dear friends we don't get to see as much as we'd like.

The ranch is a worshipful, sacred place... especially at Christmas. Over the holidays we invariably spend a great deal of time singing — two of the fellows bring their guitars

and my husband breaks out his mandolin or fiddle and they jam while the rest of us sing along.

Spending Christmas at the ranch helps us reflect on what the season is truly all about. We have a stronger focus on devotions, prayer and intimacy with God than we usually do in our hectic, everyday lives. In Hosea 2:14 it says: *"...I will allure her, I will bring her into the wilderness, and speak tenderly to her."* At Rancho Monte Nido I can truly hear the Lord speak tenderly to me — I can't think of a better way to celebrate His birth.

Christmas is not in tinsel and lights and outward show.
The secret lies in an inner glow. It's lighting a fire inside the heart.
Good will and joy a vital part. It's higher thought and a greater plan.
It's glorious dream in the soul of man.

Wilfred A. Peterson

MIKE
SWEENEY

MAJOR LEAGUE BASEBALL PLAYER
(Photo Credit: MLB photos)

Mike Sweeney made his Major League Baseball debut in September of 1995. A first baseman/designated hitter, Sweeney has spent his entire pro career as a member of the Kansas City Royals. He made the American League All-Star team five times (2000, 2001, 2002, 2003, and 2005). To date, Sweeney has compiled a .302 batting average, hit 184 home runs, and has 772 RBIs to his credit in 1,168 games. He and his wife founded The Mike and Shara Sweeney Family Foundation, a nonprofit organization devoted to bringing young people closer to Christ (www.mikesweeney.org).

Every Christmas Eve we all piled in the family van and went to my grandparent's house for a huge celebration. My mom is an O'Shea, and comes from a very large family. Not only did my grandparents have ten children, but my great-grandmother and my mentally challenged great-aunt lived with them as well. My own immediate family was large too; I had seven brothers and sisters. I also have more than thirty cousins, so altogether there was a real houseful. Our Christmas Eve celebrations were always very large and very festive. To me it was heaven on earth. Oh man, it was fun!

Everyone arrived at Grandma's and Grandpa's house around 5:00 p.m. We'd visit for a while and then have dinner. There was always a huge pot of mashed potatoes, and either a turkey or a huge roast. I can still picture my grandpa O'Shea sharpening the cutting knives to do the carving. It was a potluck, so there was a massive table full of different side dishes and desserts. And we always had deviled eggs in the house.

After dinner the kids knew it was time to open gifts. Somehow, my grandparents found a way to buy something special for each of the 30+ grandchildren, a feat that has always amazed me!

When the packages were all opened and we had finished hugging one another, the whole family caravanned to midnight mass at St. Justin Martyr Church. One of the sweetest memories I have is going to that special service. There were so many of us that we literally filled up four or five rows of pews.

The service always included offering one another the sign of God's peace. Usually it was a handshake, but our family took it to the next level and gave hugs and kisses too. After a moment, the priest went on with the service and prepared for communion, but the 40 or 50 O'Shea's and Sweeney's would still be hugging and kissing.

Probably my favorite Christmas ever was the Christmas of 1985. After a long day, the kids were pretty beat, so on the way home from mass we slept in the van. By the time we got home it was around 2:00 in the morning. We had a really large Christmas tree that year, probably 15 or 16 feet, and I remember walking through the door early that Christmas morning and noticing there were no gifts under the tree. I was about 12 years old that year, so I knew there was no Santa, yet I remember hoping there

would be a couple of gifts under the tree when we got out of bed later that morning.

Now being older, and a parent myself, I can appreciate that from 2:00 in the morning when the kids went to bed until about 6:30 when the young kids woke up, my parents were busy putting bikes together and setting gifts out. They must have been exhausted!

My parents always had a rule that we couldn't open our gifts on Christmas morning until everyone was out of bed. The young kids in the family usually got up first and woke all of the older siblings. When we woke up that particular Christmas morning, the living room was littered with gifts. But before we could open then, we placed baby Jesus in the manger of our nativity scene and my mom read the Christmas story from the Gospel of Luke.

Then we tore into our gifts. My little brother Richard and I were best friends, and that year for Christmas we got matching BMX bikes. I can still remember going out with him riding the streets on our new bikes. We felt like we were on top of the world; it was kind of like we went through a rite of passage into manhood that day.

The Christmas of 1985 was special. We had our entire family together, including my great-grandmother who only recently passed away. We spent time worshiping the Lord and remembering what the celebration was really all about. And I got the greatest gift in the world, a neat bike that I rode beside my best friend, my brother Richard.

But the angel said to them, "Do not be afraid. I bring you good news
of great joy that will be for all the people. Today in the town of David a
Savior has been born to you; he is Christ[a] the Lord. This will be a sign
to you: You will find a baby wrapped in cloths and lying in a manger."
Suddenly a great company of the heavenly host appeared with the angel,
praising God and saying, "Glory to God in the highest,
and on earth peace to men on whom his favor rests.

Luke 2:10-14

T-BONE

ACTOR/RAP ARTIST

T-Bone is considered the godfather of Christian hip hop. Launched in 1991, T-Bone's impressive career has spawned eight solo albums, including the newly released BONE-A-FIDE. *His work has resulted in a Grammy nomination, eleven Dove nominations, and a Dove Award for his contribution to the soundtrack of the rock opera* !HERO, *with which he toured in 2003 and 2004. One of the highlights of his career was his role in the box office hit* The Fighting Temptations *in 2003. His latest film,* All You've Got, *was released in 2006 (www.houseoftbone.com).*

My most memorable Christmas isn't the one when I received the best gift, had the biggest family reunion or took the most amazing trip. In fact, it's the Christmas when I learned the hardest lesson of my childhood.

When I was six years old, I was absolutely certain I was going to get a huge Christmas gift — a brand new bicycle. My parents were heading out to go shopping one day, and I was annoyed when I found out I couldn't go along. Obviously, they didn't want me to go with because they were shopping for Christmas presents, but all I knew was that I was NOT going to stay home.

Being the little brat kid that I was, I threw a major league temper tantrum. I stood at the big living room picture window crying and complaining, but they ignored me. Finally, I started yelling and banging on the window to get their attention, "I want to go! I want to go!" I pounded on the window so hard that the next thing I knew the glass came shattering down around me in a million pieces. The whole entire window broke - and on top of that I got a nasty cut on my hand.

Needless to say, my parents were not very happy. That window ended up costing them nearly $600, which back in those days was a lot of money. Instead of getting that cool bike for Christmas, my dad put a bow on the replacement window and said, "Merry Christmas." The whole experience is kind of funny when I look back on it now, but at the time I was one sad little boy.

It's funny how life has a way of coming around full circle, because my very favorite Christmas memory has to do with a house too. A few years ago, my wife and I spent some time shopping for a new house. We looked at plots of land and various floor plans, but didn't really settle on anything.

On the sly, I found the perfect lot and started building her dream house. Then on Christmas day, I put her in the car, drove up to the front of the nearly finished house and said, "Merry Christmas!"

She was totally surprised. I can still remember the tears that flowed down her beautiful face. But they were tears of joy because she was so happy. It was so rewarding to be able to do that for her. She'd always been so faithful and done so much for me that it was a wonderful honor to do something so special for her. And I know it only happened because of God's blessing.

Do you know what I like best about this new house? It has a huge picture window ...

Christmas gift suggestions:
To your enemy, forgiveness.
To an opponent, tolerance.
To a friend, your heart.
To a customer, service.
To all, charity.
To every child, a good example.
To yourself, respect.

Oren Arnold

DR. JOHN TOWNSEND

CLINICAL PSYCHOLOGIST AND AUTHOR

Marriage and family therapist Dr. John Townsend has authored and co-authored more than 18 books, including the million selling Boundaries *which he wrote with Dr. Henry Cloud. His latest book,* Boundaries with Teens, *was released in 2006. He has been awarded three Gold Medallion awards for literary excellence, as well as the Retailers Choice award for* God Will Make a Way. *Townsend is also the co-host of the nationally syndicated radio program* New Life Live! *and cofounder of Cloud-Townsend Resources (www.cloudtownsend.com).*

One Christmas, my wife and I "punk'd" our sons just like they do on the reality television show where they pull pranks on celebrities. It was the year that Razors, which are lightweight, two-wheeled, metal scooters, were the big deal, and both our kids really wanted one. But they were in huge demand and were very

hard to find ... all the store shelves were literally empty. Consequently, people were doing everything to get them. Fortunately, after looking high and low I finally found two Razors and hid them safely away.

Then my wife and I came up with up a plan. Like many other families, on Christmas morning we open numerous small presents ending up with the most valuable gift ... the big climax. That year, the big highlight was a new shirt for each of them. Now, the shirts were nice but definitely *not* exciting.

As they were opening those last gifts, our kids could see their friends through the living room window riding up and down the street on their brand new Razors. You know how kids do that – the first thing they do on Christmas morning is play with their new toys. So all their buddies were going back and forth in front of our window on their new Christmas scooters and our kids were looking at new shirts! They were living in two distinct realities – what they wanted, and what they got.

As it turned out, the boys ended up being pretty cool

about it. They just said, "Thanks a lot" and tried to smile. I apologized and said something about the expense, and how unavailable Razors were, but they still said how much they appreciated what they had received. I was actually pretty proud of them — some good manners came through in a time of deep despair.

My wife and I couldn't look at each other without falling apart. Finally it got to be too much and we pulled out the new Razors. It was a total surprise — they went wild and started beating me up.

Before we knew it they were out on the street with all their friends and we didn't see them for the rest of the day. It was a great Christmas.

Let us keep Christmas beautiful Without a thought of greed,
That it might live forevermore To fill our every need,
That it shall not be just a day, But last a lifetime through,
The miracle of Christmastime That brings God close to you.

Ann Schultz

TAMMY
TRENT

AUTHOR AND RECORDING ARTIST

A familiar face at Women of Faith and REVOLVE conferences, Tammy Trent shares her journey through the unspeakable loss of her husband and soul mate in a tragic diving accident off the coast of Jamaica. Trent's story was documented in her recent autobiography, Learning To Breathe Again: Choosing Life *and* Finding Hope After A Shattering Loss *(W Publishing, 2004), followed by her devotional/gift book,* Beyond The Sorrow: There's Hope in the Promises of God *(J Countryman, 2005). She has also recorded four albums, including her latest,* I See Beautiful, *which was released in August 2006 (www.tammytrent.com).*

M y parents divorced when I was a young child. Because I was raised in a broken home, I missed out on some of the traditions I saw some of my friends enjoy every year — things that you do with both

parents like go out on a Saturday morning and cut down a Christmas tree. To be honest, I was very envious of other families when I was growing up.

Yet even though my parents lived apart, my mom did her best to create a family atmosphere every Christmas. For example, she always played a Christmas album by Evie, and we ran through the house singing "Come on Ring Those Bells." My brother was completely embarrassed and would never sing it with us. Mom still loves that record, but now when she wants to put it on, we all start laughing and somebody tries to hide the album.

I remember baking cookies with mom just about every Christmas and giving them away to neighbors or older people from church. We always baked some kind of sugar cookie, you know, the kind where you use cookie cutters — snowmen, stars, shepherds — and then we sprinkled them with colored sugar and other colorful decorations. Looking back on it now, I wonder who would have really wanted those things ... those cookies imprinted with grubby little fingers. But man, were we proud of them!

As an adult, I cling to certain memories I had early in my childhood — the ones when you close your eyes and are vividly taken back to a particular moment in time. Those are the memories that stick with you forever.

One such moment happened for me was when I was about 6 years old. I remember asking for a drum set for Christmas. There I was, this tiny little girl, and for whatever reason I wanted a drum set. My mom was a singer and was in bands her whole life. When I came home from school they would be practicing in the living room. I was always fascinated by the drums.

I remember waking up early that particular Christmas morning, walking downstairs by myself, peeking around the corner and seeing this beautiful red drum set. It was huge! There was a picture of Bugs Bunny on the bass drum and I thought it was the coolest thing I had ever seen in my life. I thought for sure it must have cost my parents millions of dollars.

I found some makeshift drumsticks - in the form of kitchen utensils - and proceeded to wake up the entire

family by banging on those drums. I assumed they were for my brother; it wasn't actually until my family dragged themselves out of bed that morning that I learned they belonged to me. I was so excited!

To this day, that drum set is probably one of the greatest gifts I have ever received. I don't even remember past that Christmas morning; I don't remember how long I had those drums, or what happened to them, but I will never forget waking up Christmas day to see my dream come true.

When Christmas bells are swinging above the fields of snow,
we hear sweet voices ringing from lands of long ago,
and etched on vacant places are half-forgotten faces of friends
we used to cherish, and loves we used to know.

Ella Wheeler Wilcox

KURT
WARNER

NFL PLAYER

Three-time Pro Bowl participant Kurt Warner is the quarterback for the Arizona Cardinals of the National Football League. He is a two-time NFL Most Valuable Player (1999 and 2001) and has made two appearances in the Super Bowl. He was selected MVP of Super Bowl XXXIV after leading his St. Louis Rams to victory. He and his wife Brenda created the First Things First Foundation in 2001 to share their blessings with those in need. (www.kurtwarner.org).

O ver the last four or five years, my family has developed a wonderful Christmas tradition. Every year we adopt a children's home in St. Louis; an orphanage, shelter or foster home, and help them celebrate the holiday. The administrators of the home provide us with a wish list and we have the privilege of buying gifts for the children and spending Christmas

Day with them.

My whole family goes; and for 2-3 hours each Christmas morning we sing songs and talk about Jesus and the true meaning of Christmas. One of our favorite things to do with the children is play games that get everybody involved. Overall, we just enjoy getting to know each other and having fun. We spend the car ride home and the rest of the day talking about how we were touched by our experiences.

Out of all the memories I've amassed over the course of my lifetime, these have become my favorite Christmases. Of course, I remember my favorite gifts and things growing up, but it's been awesome for me and my family to share these experiences together. I believe that's what Christ came to tell us... that we're here to serve and reach out and touch the lives of others.

I can't pinpoint one particular Christmas as being the most memorable, because each one is special in its own right. This tradition has become very rewarding for us, but has also made a difference for the kids we've visited.

One event really stands out. There was a young boy who was very withdrawn the entire time and would not interact with anyone. A staff member told us that on the ride home, he became very animated and said, "This is the best Christmas I've ever had!" They were shocked at his sudden change! He wanted to see his Bible as soon as he got in the car and said every day he would read it and pray for my pinky finger, which was injured at the time. What was so amazing about that commitment was that this twelve-year-old child read at only a kindergarten level. So for him to say he was going to read every day was very ambitious!

Many children have told us what these Christmas events have meant to them — but we're the real beneficiaries — the entire Warner family. I have seen our kids come to appreciate what they have much more than they did before. It is so easy for them to take our situation for granted: food, clothes, accessories, toys, etc... So to visit someone who doesn't live in a situation like we do is very eye-opening for them. I think our little ones believe everyone has a life like theirs and this program helps to open their eyes to the reality of the world around them.

It is fun to watch the kids go from being shy and not wanting to be there, to making friends and not wanting to leave. Our kids have come to realize that even though these kids don't have what we have they are really just like us on the inside. That can be something we all forget.

I'll admit it, sometimes I say to myself on Christmas morning, "Do I really want to leave my home and spend Christmas with strangers?" But, it only takes a couple of minutes with these special kids to realize this program is the highlight of our day. It is so awesome to see people who are truly appreciative of being blessed on Christmas. They understand that without the help of others their Christmas would be simply like any other day – and we never want anyone to feel like Christmas is just another day.

Through this service project, our kids have been introduced to what Christmas is really about... giving. Not just the giving of gifts, but giving the love of Jesus to all those with whom we come in contact. Of all we do, the giving of ourselves is the greatest reminder of what Jesus came to do for us on that first Christmas Day. We're blessed beyond measure to share Jesus' birthday with His children.

*Christmas is most truly Christmas when we celebrate it
by giving the light of love to those who need it most.*

Ruth Carter Stapleton

MIKE WEAVER

RECORDING ARTIST —
BIG DADDY WEAVE

Contemporary Christian band Big Daddy Weave's first project, One and Only, *debuted on SoundScan's Christian Top 5, the highest debut for a new artist in 2002. That year they also received a Gospel Music Association Dove Award nomination for "New Artist of the Year." Their single, "Audience of One," was the band's first number one song (*Christian Radio Weekly *CHR chart) and they have since gone on to earn 4 more top 4 singles.* Every Time I Breathe, *their latest project, was released in September 2006.*

This past Christmas was my first one as a married man. It was this year that I really got to know a lot of my wife's extended family, especially the men. Being the new guy is kind of a scary thing, and I've had some situations in my life before where I was the new guy and it really didn't go that great for me. But this time,

it was different. Her family was so kind and they totally loved me. That meant a lot — especially to be accepted by the other guys. They all made me feel welcome.

Now that we're married, holidays are more complicated. Like so many other couples, we are on a yearly rotation between families. But this year, we got to spend time with both groups; we celebrated an early Christmas with her family and spent Christmas Day with my folks.

The way each family celebrates the holidays is completely different. Growing up it was just the two of us, Mike and Jay. I mean the Weaver brothers broke the mold! When we were kids, we always went to Grandma's house. In my earlier years, I usually just kind of escaped and sat in the back room of her house and played the guitar. In fact, some of the songs from our first record come out of that room on just such occasions when the house seemed a little bit too full.

But if it is just immediate family, our Christmas is very laid back. There's no real sense of order, we just kind of hang out together. And if we get around to it, we open presents. We don't have very many rituals in our family; even the opening of presents is casual – oftentimes they're not even be wrapped!

It was like night and day when we went to Kandice's family Christmas celebration. At her place, there is definitely a set order of things. First we have dinner. At Nana Ruth's house, it's an unbelievable buffet... I mean this is home cooked, real stuff. There are lots of pies and cakes and cookies; things that big daddies probably shouldn't be eating.

After dinner, we start with the opening of presents. The guys wait, because we're supposed to be gentlemen I guess, and the ladies go first. The adults in Kandice's family do a gift exchange

We do the exchange as a game, trading presents until each of us winds up with a gift. The men all just bring gift cards, so I, of course, brought an iTunes gift card. I'm a huge fan of iPods, iTunes and Apple computers and I had to play really hard – and just a little bit dirty – to make sure I got it back. But in the end, I took the iTunes home!

A Christmas Blessing

God grant you the light of Christmas, which is faith; the warmth of Christmas, which is love; the radiance of Christmas, which is purity; the righteousness of Christmas, which is justice; the belief in Christmas, which is truth; the all of Christmas, which is Christ.

Wilda English

GLEN WESLEY

NHL PLAYER
(Photo: Carolina Hurricanes)

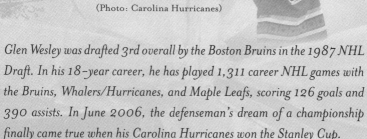

Glen Wesley was drafted 3rd overall by the Boston Bruins in the 1987 NHL Draft. In his 18-year career, he has played 1,311 career NHL games with the Bruins, Whalers/Hurricanes, and Maple Leafs, scoring 126 goals and 390 assists. In June 2006, the defenseman's dream of a championship finally came true when his Carolina Hurricanes won the Stanley Cup.

I left home when I was only 15 years old to play junior hockey. My mom wasn't really too pleased, but she knew my dream was to play professional hockey. Three years later, I was drafted by the Boston Bruins and my dream came true. My life changed dramatically after that — I no longer lived in Canada with the rest of my family and was always on the road. My rookie year was the last year we all got to spend Christmas together for more than a decade.

In 1999, I flew my whole family — my mom, my brothers, sisters and their families — to Raleigh for the holidays. Most of them came in from Alberta, and they all stayed with us; we had close to 20 people in our house. To be able to spend that time with them was very special because it hadn't happened in such a long time. It was very memorable to say the least.

With our own kids, we are trying to carry on a tradition from my wife's childhood. On Christmas Eve we read some sort of devotional Christmas story together and then we make homemade pizza. It's a great activity because it's something we can all do together. And since my wife lost her mother, it's a way for us to bring a little piece of her into the next generation.

For unto us a child is born, to us a son is given, and the government
will be on his shoulders. And he will be called Wonderful Counselor,
Mighty God, Everlasting Father, Prince of Peace.

Isaiah 9:6

DAVID
WHEATON

AUTHOR AND PROFESSIONAL
TENNIS PLAYER

In the 1990's, David Wheaton was one of the top tennis players in the world. During his 13 years on the pro tennis tour, the Minnesota native competed regularly against tennis greats like Pete Sampras, Andre Agassi, Jim Courier, Michael Chang, Ivan Lendl, and Boris Becker. Semi-retired from professional tennis, in 2004 he claimed the Wimbledon Over-35 Doubles championship title. Wheaton now hosts a Christian radio show, is a motivational speaker, and is the author of University of Destruction — Your Game Plan for Spiritual Victory on Campus *(www.davidwheaton.com).*

I come from Minnesota, the land of 10,000 lakes, where many people say we have only two seasons: winter and three months of tough sledding. Life in the upper Midwest doesn't stop because of the snow and cold temperatures — it's actually just the opposite. Most

237

Minnesotans find ways to not only survive the long cold winter, but to revel in it: ice skating, downhill and cross country skiing, snowmobiling and hockey are just a few popular activities.

To people living in warmer climates, one of our quirkiest activities is probably ice fishing. Because of the length of our winters and the cold temperatures, most lakes freeze over in the winter. By December you'll see entire communities spring up on area lakes with fish houses that boast sleeping accommodations, heaters and even televisions so avid fans won't miss that big Vikings game. There are even plowed "roads" that emerge between these little villages.

When I was a kid growing up on Lake Minnetonka, the 10th largest lake in the state, my favorite winter activity was going out on the lake with our two Siberian Huskies, "Tonka" and "Tinka."

(David, 7 and "Tonka")

Being just one step removed from wolves, Huskies are definitely wilder than most other breeds. Consequently, they love to run and require lots of exercise. When I was a boy, I had a couple of harnesses that I would attach to the dogs and then to my lightweight plastic sled. I'd jump on my stomach and they would pull me around out on the lake to the ice fishing villages. There were roads between them, but no real traffic, so we could rip from place to place. The byways were a little bit icy, so we would be running at quite a clip. Once I put the harnesses on those huskies, they would just tear across the lake.

My most memorable Christmas was when I was about 12 years old. As usual, we had Christmas as a family at my parents' house that year. We read about the birth of Jesus from the book of Luke, sang some Christmas carols and opened presents.

When we had finished opening up our presents, my parents told me they had one more special gift for me and directed me to look out the window. There on the front lawn in a blanket of freshly fallen snow was a hand-made dog sled! My parents had commissioned a dog sled maker

to custom-design a one-of-a-kind, two-dog dog sled. This was the real thing.

I was thrilled out of my mind! It was such a unique gift and really caught my imagination as a child. I loved my dogs and loved being with them out on the lake, so it couldn't have been any better. It wasn't a toy or a game for a little kid... this was a unique grown-up present that I still have to this day.

We just flew on in that sled. Tonka and Tinka weren't highly trained to pull and they didn't really follow any commands or anything like that, but all you had to do was point them in the right direction and they'd take off. The three of us had grand adventures in the formative years of my boyhood.

More than twenty-five years later, I still have that dog sled as a keepsake in my home. Although I don't do much mushing these days, and my huskies are long gone, that sled is still a beautiful piece of artwork overflowing with memories. Every time I see it I remember my favorite Christmas.

Heap on more wood!
The wind is chill;
But let it whistle
As it will.
We'll keep
Our Christmas
Merry still

Sir Walter Scott

JACKLYN ZEMAN

ACTRESS
(Photo Courtesy of ABC)

Jacklyn Zeman has played nurse Bobbie Spencer on the ABC daytime drama **General Hospital** *for 29 seasons and has more than 4,000 episodes to her credit. Her achievements have included four Daytime Emmy nominations, a Soap Opera Digest Award, and the Hollywood International Favorite Actress Award. Zeman has also guest starred on several television series, including "Chicago Hope," "Mike Hammer," and "Love, American Style," and is a frequent guest of television talk shows and game shows.*

To me, the important, most wonderful part of Christmas is the love and the family and the tradition of it. It's all about establishing traditions and memories for our children and ourselves that will live on over the years. And we have a lot of tradition in our family when it comes to Christmas.

Probably my favorite Christmas memory was when my

girls were little; Lacey was two and Cassidy was four. We went to New Jersey that year, because that's where my mom lived, along with my two sisters and their families.

Back in those days, we started cooking three days ahead. I was the baker, because I like pies and cakes and sweets. My sister, Carol, is like an Italian maven, so she made the lasagna or the pasta. My sister Lauren likes hors d'oeuvres so she made this incredible sausage bread that everybody just loves. My mother made the main course; it was always a home style family meal with potatoes and gravy.

Our big celebration started on Christmas Eve. We had an early dinner with the kids, and then walked two blocks to Old South Presbyterian Church. We all had our nice clothes on; the women wore long skirts or something velvet, and our best jewelry. I dressed my girls up that year too, they had their special little red dresses on with flowers all over them and wore sparkly shoes. They felt very fancy and grown up.

The journey to church was magical. As was tradition, for several blocks the sidewalk was lined with luminaria

- glowing candles placed inside paper bags. The most beautiful candlelight lit our path all the way up the walkway to the front door of the building. It looked just like how I picture heaven. To this day, I can see it in my mind.

After the service, we walked back home and enjoyed our lavish smorgasbord that mom spread out on the coffee table. Then the whole family exchanged gifts. That year was a particularly wonderful year because it was something of a crossroads. My girls were finally old enough to *get* Christmas, to really understand what was going on. They were able to think in terms of not only what they were going to get, but what they were going to give. In fact, they each made a beautiful hand-painted mug that year, and gave one to their dad and one to me. Nearly 12 years later, I'm still using mine every morning.

That Christmas was also a great time for the cousins to bond, and really spend time together. There was snow on the ground, so the next day we took out the flying saucers and a little sled and took them sledding. Then we all laid in the yard and made snow angels and built snowmen. There's something so picturesque when there's snow on

the ground and the big old trees are strung with icicles. My kids grew up in California, so the only time they see snow is when we go back to New Jersey for Christmas. I love the fact that they got to see that and experience that.

As I looked out the kitchen window of my childhood home that Christmas Day, I was filled with fond memories of playing in the backyard. And I was filled with gratitude for the gift of my own little girls. What a blessing it has been to help them create their own memories.

I'm dreaming of a white Christmas
Just like the ones I used to know
Where the treetops glisten,
and children listen
To hear sleigh bells in the snow

I'm dreaming of a white Christmas
With every Christmas card I write
May your days be merry and bright
And may all your Christmases be white

Irving Berlin

ZORO

MUSICIAN AND
MOTIVATIONAL SPEAKER

Zoro the Drummer is an internationally known rock star and Christian ambassador. One of the world's most renowned and respected drummers, he has toured and recorded with Lenny Kravitz, Bobby Brown, Frankie Valli and the Four Seasons, The New Edition, Jody Watley, Sean Lennon, Lisa Marie Presley, and many others. The voice of a generation, Zoro speaks at churches, schools, conferences, youth groups, and corporate events all over the world. Zoro is passionate about impacting the lives of children and is a spokesperson for Compassion International, a Christian child advocacy ministry (www.zorothedrummer.com).

There were seven kids in my family, and we were all raised by a single mother. She was from Mexico City originally, and we didn't have any extended family here in the United States — no grandparents, uncles, or aunts.

My mother, Maria, had some significant health issues, including debilitating arthritis, which made it impossible for her to hold down a job. Consequently, we were a welfare family living off food stamps and barely getting by. And because of that, Christmas was a real struggle for my mother. Yet she did her best to make it special.

(Zoro, Bobby and Lisa)

Music was always playing in our house, and at Christmastime we had the old standards on the turntable: Nat King Cole, Elvis, Johnny Mathis, and Perry Como to name a few. Every Christmas we also listened to Perry Como's narration of the classic holiday poem, *The Night Before Christmas*. It was something we looked forward to every year.

As a family, we gathered around the television every season to watch those timeless Christmas movies. One of my favorites was the 1970 musical *Scrooge,* starring Albert Finney and Sir Alec Guinness. Then there was *Miracle on 34th Street, How The Grinch Stole Christmas, It's a Wonderful Life, Frosty the Snowman,* and the "claymation" films *Rudolph the Red Nosed Reindeer* and *Santa Claus is Coming to Town* with Burl Ives and Fred Astaire.

Like most kids, my brothers and sisters and I spent a lot of time dreaming about what we wanted for Christmas. Every year we took turns looking through the Montgomery Wards and Sears Wishbook catalogs dreaming of things we could never have. I remember my brother, Bobby, and I sitting side by side with the catalog on our laps pretending that we were getting everything on our side of the page for Christmas. It was a fun way of dreaming and imagining.

Because we were so economically challenged, my mother had to be creative to make ends meet and still give us a merry Christmas. One way she accomplished that was by signing up for community programs. For example, the Jaycees, a nonprofit youth development organization, had

a program that provided poor children with $10 so they could buy presents for their families.

Mom also visited the local fire department and took advantage of their Toys for Tots drive. Every Christmas Eve they came through with a basket of toys for us. One year they brought Lincoln Logs and that was the biggest thrill ever. When I got them on Christmas morning I set them up a thousand different ways.

Now when I think about my favorite Christmas memory, one in particular really jumps out. As a kid I loved to bang on things — coffee cans or whatever I could get my hands on. But for years I had wanted a real drum set. Every time I looked in the Sears Wishbook and came across the page with the drums on it, that's all I could focus on. But obviously, I knew there was no way that was going to happen.

But one Christmas morning when I looked under the tree, there was an enormous box with my name on it. I remember ripping that box open and finding a whole drum set in it. I can still picture exactly what it looked like — it had a picture of Mickey Mouse on the bass drum. My reaction was one of pure and total elation. The only way I can describe it is that I was overflowing with joy. You know the feeling; when you have your heart set on something and you finally get it, the feeling is pretty awesome. Believe it or not, I think my mom had more joy than I did just watching me open it up, because it had taken everything she had to be to able to get it for me.

I banged happily on that drum set all Christmas Day and night until it broke. The skins were made of paper, so I ripped right through them. But even though it was destroyed, it set a fire in me. I believe that particular Christmas changed my destiny. Fortunately, my mom lived long enough to see what happened with that one little seed she planted.

Now I have children of my own. And since they were toddlers I've taught them what the word compassion means. One Christmas I took them to Toys "R" Us and told them to pick out what they wanted the most for Christmas. Of course, they both picked out the biggest, coolest thing they could find.

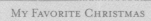

Then I said, "I'm not going to give those toys to you... we're going to take them to the fire department and put them in the big Toys for Tots bin and bless somebody else." I explained that there were people in our community who didn't have money to buy presents, so we were going to give those children our presents and make them the happiest kids in the world.

Then I said, "When I was a little boy, I was one of those children. If it weren't for the fire department I wouldn't have had something big and special." I was the kid on Christmas Day who got something great because of the generosity of strangers.

When I took my kids to the fire department that day, the firefighters were really enamored with them. Little kids didn't usually come in and donate the gifts themselves. As a reward, my kids were given a private tour of the fire station and got to sit on the fire engine and even put the headphones on. It was like a bonus I hadn't counted on from teaching them how to give. They were blessed because they gave from their hearts and God showed them His favor. It was a great lesson.

We do that every year now — it has become our special family tradition. Because of that experience, my kids have become real givers. Last year I went on a mission trip to Ghana. When I returned and showed my kids the photos from my trip, my little boy said something that just blew me away. One of the little African boys in the pictures was missing a finger, and my five—year-old son asked me how much a finger cost. He wanted to buy a new one for that little African boy for Christmas! Tears poured down my cheeks because I knew my son understood what compassion was really all about. And that's the true meaning of Christmas.

We consider Christmas as the encounter, the great encounter, the
historical encounter, the decisive encounter, between God and mankind.
He who has faith knows this truly; let him rejoice.

Pope Paul VI